oct 16, 2017

Dear Diane,

Looking forward further
learning opportunities
with you!

Byoungheo Jin

Palgrave Studies in Practice: Global Fashion Brand Management

Series Editors
Byoungho Jin
Department of Consumer, Apparel and Retail Studies
Bryan School of Business and Economics
The University of North Carolina
Greensboro, NC, USA

Elena Cedrola
Department of Economics and Law
University of Macerata
Macerata, Italy

Branding and internationalization are critical aspects of any business, and the fashion industry is especially global in nature. Very few apparel items are entirely produced within one country, and it is relatively easier for fashion brands to enter international markets because little financial investment is required, small-scale retail space is possible, and economies of scale can be maximized. Accordingly, there are more successful internationalization cases in the fashion industry than any other sector, yet no one text handles these critical topics (i.e., branding and internationalization) in one book, particularly in case study format. This series will focus on fashion brand cases that have been successful in global marketplaces. By examining their strategies in diverse aspects such as internationalization, innovation, branding and communication, and retail management, these books will help students, scholars, and practitioners grasp lesser-known yet effective international marketing strategies.

More information about this series at
http://www.springer.com/series/14598

Byoungho Jin • Elena Cedrola
Editors

Fashion Branding and Communication

Core Strategies of European Luxury Brands

Editors
Byoungho Jin
Department of Consumer, Apparel
 and Retail Studies
Bryan School of Business
 and Economics
The University of North Carolina
Greensboro, NC, USA

Elena Cedrola
Department of Economics and Law
University of Macerata
Macerata, Italy

Palgrave Studies in Practice: Global Fashion Brand Management
ISBN 978-1-137-52342-6   ISBN 978-1-137-52343-3 (eBook)
DOI 10.1057/978-1-137-52343-3

Library of Congress Control Number: 2017930191

Cover illustration: Détail de la Tour Eiffel © nemesis2207/Fotolia.co.uk

Printed on acid-free paper

This Palgrave Pivot imprint is published by Springer Nature
The registered company is Nature America Inc.
The registered company address is: 1 New York Plaza, New York, NY 10004, U.S.A.

To my parents who taught me the virtues of diligence, justice, and sincerity
BJ

To the great women in my life: Rosalba, Elena, Elena, and Caterina.
EC

MORE PRAISE FOR *FASHION BRANDING AND COMMUNICATION*

"This book exposes best-practices in luxury and fashion industries that have expanded globally whilst remaining true to their DNA. It illustrates the importance of strategic consistency in time and across countries. It is an inspiration for marketers in the luxury and fashion industries."

–Dr. Marie-Cécile Cervellon, Professor of Marketing,
EDHEC Business School, France

"A well-balanced content and a set-up that feels modern and up to date on the subject. The book's way of allowing the reader to follow corporate thoughts create a broad understanding of how the fashion industry works. It is also a very educational tool for understanding the complexity of the fashion industry."

–Dr. Håkan Preiholt, Stockholm Business School,
Stockholm University, Sweden

"An interesting volume that points out challenges and trends in branding and communication in the fashion industry. All the case studies selected are real milestones for practitioners and, of course, Master's and MBA students."

–Dr. Carlo Arlotta, Partner, Consilia Business Management,
Milan, Italy

PREFACE

Every firm dreams of creating a well-established brand. Especially for fashion companies, brand name is a paramount concern, often serving as a deciding factor for consumer purchase decisions. Consumers do not necessarily seek functionality in fashion. Instead, they purchase styles, dreams, and symbolic images—aspects of their identity that brands can help them project. Therefore, in the fashion industry, brand is a critical asset many firms strive to establish, maintain, and grow. The study of branding is complex because no single factor plays a decisive role in its development. To elucidate this intricate subject, we chose to structure this book around case studies, building on previous works on branding. In particular, we focus on European luxury and premium brands because of its massive influence on branding and communication. Luxury strategies have their roots in Europe, primarily pioneered by French and Italian companies. This book specifically focuses on four Italian companies (Harmont & Blaine, Salvatore Ferragamo, Tod's, and Prada) and one French company (Louis Vuitton). Each case was written by author(s) who have either come from the region, provided marketing consultation for the brands, or conducted in-depth studies of the brands. Their connections provided us with invaluable access to interviews with executives and reviews of archives would have been otherwise limited. These experiences have allowed us to write this text, compiled from information not easily obtainable elsewhere.

This book begins with an overview chapter, creating a backdrop to help facilitate a holistic understanding of the five cases. The chapter introduces major brands and communication-related concepts with a particular focus on prominent fashion brands in Europe and America. The objective of the first chapter is not to summarize the concepts of branding and communication. On the contrary, the chapter has two specific aims. First, it addresses aspects of branding and communication that have often been overlooked in previous studies. In particular, we highlight fashion industries in Western continents, discussing specific examples and practices from companies in this region. Second, this chapter describes major challenges and changes in the industry. This will create a foundation for readers to understand the five subsequent chapters, as these challenges and trends will reappear throughout the cases in this text.

The five cases in this book are diverse in their brand portfolio management and their focus on brand communication. Though they were not chosen for their similarities, they nonetheless strikingly resemble each other. First, all five cases hold a tight control over the quality of their products through various measures and continuous innovation within the company. Ferragamo's patent on shoes is an example of this. To control their quality, Harmont & Blaine and Ferragamo manufacture mainly in Italy, employing small workshops and in-house facilities. In fact, a majority of these companies started in workshops in small towns. These experiences have cultivated in the companies a spirit of craftsmanship that will remain for generations to come. Second, all five cases were forerunners in the fashion industry in their decision to expand internationally and extend their brands. Only a little more than two decades after its establishment, Harmont & Blaine (Chapter 2) currently exports to 50 countries with approximately 20% of their sales revenue coming from exports. Ferragamo (Chapter 3) and Tod's (Chapter 4) earn 80% and 70% of their sales revenue, respectively, from exports. In the case of Prada (Chapter 5) and of Louis Vuitton (Chapter 6), about 90% and 86% of their sales revenue, respectively, stem from exports. Ferragamo has expanded to 99 countries, and Tod's has extended to 37. Third, all five brands have their roots in a family, and their descendants still operate the brands, passing down the company from generation to generation. This form of ownership has been instrumental in keeping family philosophy and brand heritage alive. Fourth, these companies value long-term partnerships with subcontractors, leadership in corporate social responsibilities, and dedication to the community. Collectively, these morals have helped shape their corporate image and commitment to product quality. Fifth, these companies have developed innovative de-commodization strategies though each brand's strategy is unique—Ferragamo through corporate museums and exhibitions (Chapter 3), Tod's storytelling via Princess

Diana and Jacqueline Kennedy (Chapter 4), Prada's cutting-edge Epicenters through a collaboration with renowned architect (Chapter 5), and Louis Vuitton's artification strategies via collaborations with leading Japanese artists (Chapter 6).

These cases demonstrate how a family workshop from a small town can grow into a global luxury or premium brand within a relatively short amount of time. Their ability to do so was not a consequence of marketing and branding effort alone. Rather, the combination of their brand strategies and their enthusiasm for their products pushed these companies to this level of success. These firms demonstrate that branding is most effective when it is first rooted in a commitment to quality. Many small firms emerge and disappear every day. Branding and communication are key for companies to continue to grow. As such, we hope that the strategies in this book provide inspiration and practical insight for firms striving to reach their potential.

In that sense, this book is a useful read not only to undergraduate and graduate students but also practitioners in the industries of fashion, retailing, branding, and international business. Scholars who conduct research branding and communication in the fashion industry will also benefit from this text as we review literature and explore examples across Europe and America.

This book would not be possible without the support of many people. We extend our deepest gratitude to executives and marketing communication directors of the five companies in this text who took time from their busy schedules to share their stories with us and to review earlier drafts. Their insight and vision will inspire many more business executives to come. We express special thanks to authors of each chapter who conducted multiple interviews with key informants, traveled to headquarters, museums, and associations to collect visual images and archives, and consolidated the insightful information with great dedication. Their contribution was even more meaningful as the information was in multiple languages: French, Italian, and English. We were fortunate to have the support of former and current research assistants. A particular thanks to Naeun (Lauren) Kim for finding information for the book and checking formats and references across the cases. We also thank Anna Chiappelli for obtaining information and assisting with the bibliometric analysis.

Greensboro, NC, USA   Byoungho Jin
Macerata, Italy   Elena Cedrola

CONTENTS

LIST OF FIGURES

LIST OF TABLES

CHAPTER 1

Brands as Core Assets: Trends and Challenges of Branding in Fashion Business

Byoungho Jin and Elena Cedrola

Abstract The importance of brand in the fashion business cannot be overemphasized. This chapter reviews the essence of fashion brand management, discussing the concepts of brand and brand equity, fashion brand development and management, and communication. The fashion brand communication section introduces the use of emergent social media and fashion blogs along with traditional media in the luxury and premium fashion industry. Challenges and trends in branding and communication in the fashion industry are also discussed. The challenges around luxury brands, such as counterfeit goods, commoditization, brand dilution, and brand avoidance are explained with prominent examples. In the subsequent section, trends in branding and communication are detailed: luxury

B. Jin (✉)
Department of Consumer, Apparel and Retail Studies,
Bryan School of Business and Economics, University of North Carolina,
Greensboro, NC, USA

E. Cedrola
Department of Economics and Law, University of Macerata,
Macerata, Italy

© The Author(s) 2017
B. Jin, E. Cedrola (eds.), *Fashion Branding and Communication*,
Palgrave Studies in Practice: Global Fashion Brand Management,
DOI 10.1057/978-1-137-52343-3_1

1

brands' offering online selling, limited edition, guerrilla marketing, pop-up stores, reinforcing brand equity by offering experiential spaces. Major concepts are explained using examples to help readers understand the larger scope of the topic, which will be instrumental in understanding branding strategies of five European luxury and premium brands cases in this volume.

Keywords Fashion brand · Brand equity · Brand portfolio · Brand extension · Brand communication

INTRODUCTION

The most important asset a fashion company maintains is its brand. A constellation of assets is required to operate a firm: a building, a factory, an office, a store, an owner, employees, a brand, skills, patents, etc. Most of these assets are replaceable—the building, factory, offices, employees, and even owners can be changed. Factories may not be even needed as many fashion firms such as Gap, Inc., Nike, and Armani operate their businesses without owning production facilities at all. Brands, however, are forever. For well-known global brands, the value of brand may be far greater than all tangible assets (e.g., building, factory, offices, stores, etc.) combined. The value of a brand, oftentimes referred to as "brand asset," is expressed in cash value. According to Interbrand (2015),[1] the highest brand asset is Apple, valued at USD $170,276 million. The second highest is Google at $120,314 million, followed by Coca-Cola, Microsoft, and IBM. Among fashion brands, Louis Vuitton ranked 20th in the same list and H&M ranked 21st valued at $22,250 and $22,222 million, respectively—close to the GDP of Estonia in 2015! The importance of brand is obvious. Typical operational margin for an OEM (Original Equipment Manufacturer) is approximately 2 % but can be as high as 30 % for globally branded firms like Apple, Inc. (Kumar & Steenkamp, 2013).

Brand asset is valuable in every business, but it becomes critical in the fashion industry where most assets are non-tangible. A company's reliance on non-tangible assets can be evaluated by examining its Q ratio, or the share of a company's value that stems from non-tangibles such as brand and innovation. According to the National Retail Federation, the Q ratio is greatest in apparel/footwear sectors, with French luxury goods company Hermès holding the highest value (National Retail Federation, 2016). The high Q ratio in apparel/footwear sectors is partly due to difficulty in judging the quality of these products in comparison to electronic goods and cars—as brand and image primarily drive the quality judgment of apparel/footwear (Kumar & Steenkamp, 2013). Moreover, due to low entry barriers, fashion brands are in competition. Brand can serve as the single most important criterion for purchase decisions among many consumers.

Brands are strategically managed at the center of fashion companies. With the advances in technology and popularity of social media, fashion firms are rapidly improving their branding and communication endeavors. Following an introduction of the concepts of brand, brand assets, brand classifications, and basics of brand development and management process, this chapter will introduce both traditional and emerging methods of brand communication in the context of the fashion industry. Finally, this chapter details the challenges and trends in brand and communication using examples of global fashion brands.

CONCEPTS AND CLASSIFICATION OF BRAND

Brand and Brand Equity

The brand is an essential part of the buying process because it is a sum of tangible and non-tangible elements that allow consumers to quickly learn about the intrinsic characteristics of a product and the quality of the producer. The brand communicates the non-tangible attributes and stylistic codes of an offer, using a set of symbols, to provoke certain emotions (Ciappei & Surchi, 2011). As such, the evocative and symbolic elements of the product tend to prevail over functionality, distinguishing the offer from others. This strategic value of a brand is referred to as "brand equity."

David Aaker, in his book *Managing Brand Equity*, coins the term "brand equity," defining it as "a set of brand assets and liabilities linked to a brand name and symbol, which add to or subtract from the value provided by a product or service" (Aaker, 1991, p. 15). Connecting brand to the concept of "equity" and "assets" radically changed the marketing function, allowing it to extend beyond conventional strategies. Brand equity provides value for the firm by enhancing the efficiency and effectiveness of marketing programs and providing higher margins for products through premium pricing and decreased reliance on promotions. It also provides a platform for growth through brand extensions, which will be explained later in detail.

At the same time, brand equity improves the consumer experience, enhancing their ability to interpret and process information and improving confidence in their purchase decision (Aaker, 1992).

Aaker created a model that describes how brand equity generates value for a firm, which includes four dimensions: brand loyalty, brand awareness, brand associations, and perceived quality. Brand loyalty measures people's loyalty to a brand. Loyal customers are less sensitive to competitors' price and other factors, presenting a significant entry barrier to competitors. Brand loyalty also helps reduce marketing costs since retaining loyal customers costs less than acquiring new ones, making it the ultimate goal for many companies. Brand awareness is the extent to which a brand is known by the public and the associations triggered by the brand. Perceived quality refers to the extent to which a brand is considered to provide quality products. Other proprietary assets include patents, intellectual property rights, and relations with trade partners. The more proprietary assets a brand has accumulated, the greater the brand's competitive edge exists (Aaker, 1991).

Fashion Brand Classification

In the fashion industry, brands can be identified using various parameters. Depending on target segments or the positioning strategy, brands can be classified into four categories: *griffe*, luxury brands, premium brands, and mass-market brands (Hameide, 2011). Fig. 1.1 summarizes the production process and the value expressed in each category. As Fig. 1.1 shows, the higher the price range, the narrower the target audience as fewer people can afford it.

Griffe, or designer brand, is at the top of the pyramid. The term *griffe* is derived from handwriting and refers to the pure creation of an item by hand, created in *atelier*. Thus, it is unique, irreproducible, and eternal. Yves Saint Laurent is an example of *griffe* (Kapferer, 1999). Some famous designer brands oftentimes also offer luxury brands—Dior produces both *griffe* and luxury brands.

The next brand category in Fig. 1.1 is luxury brand, which originates from either designer brands (e.g., Dior and Chanel) or craftsmanship (e.g., Gucci and Louis Vuitton). Luxury brand has six features: excellent quality, high price, scarcity and uniqueness, aesthetics and poly-sensuality, ancestral heritage and personal history, and superfluousness (Dubois, Laurent, & Czellar, 2001). The essential elements of luxury products are craft, uniqueness, exclusivity, and artistic talent—though some crafts have been replaced by machines. Luxury

Fig. 1.1 The classification of fashion brands (*Note*: Adapted from Kapferer (2008), p. 98)

brands offer excellent quality, scarcity and uniqueness, and excellent aesthetics and poly-sensuality—all of which claim these products a high price.

Luxury brands are also characterized by its ancestral heritage, personal and cultural history, and geographical roots (Kapferer & Bastien, 2010). Many luxury brands have a long history (Table 1.1), and their present artisanal heritage is closely linked to its cultural patrimony—such as English classicism and tailoring, Italian Romanticism, and French couture and artistry (Kapferer & Bastien, 2010). Luxury brands, such as Salvatore Ferragamo, have some personal history as well. Chapter 3 of this volume on Ferragamo illustrates how the name of Salvatore Ferragamo becomes both the name of a brand and a company.

The last characteristic of luxury brand is its superfluousness. Luxury brands are often described as those "brands that no one really needs, but everyone desires" (Hameide, 2011, p. 110). Originally, luxury items were made for royalty, aristocracy, and the upper class until the nineteenth century. As such, luxury brands have a strong connotation of success, allowing consumers to attain a privileged social standing through these items.

The third brand category in Fig. 1.1 is premium brand. Also called new luxury or new luxe, premium brands have elements from both luxury and mass-market brands. "They are at the top of the mass-market spectrum concerning price, yet at the same time they are more accessible than luxury brands" (Hameide, 2011, p. 26). Premium brands have refined their products

Table 1.1   The established year of leading luxury brands

Year of foundation	*Brands*
1837	Hermès
1847	Cartier
1856	Burberry
1854	Louis Vuitton
1913	Prada
1915	Chanel
1919	Balenciaga
1921	Gucci
1925	Fendi
1927	Salvatore Ferragamo
1945	Pierre Balmain
1946	Christian Dior
1952	Hubert de Givency
1960	Valentino
1962	Yves Saint Laurent
1965	Emanuel Ungaro
1966	Bottega Veneta
1975	Giorgio Armani
1976	Jean-Paul Gaultier
1978	Versace
1987	Christian Lacroix

Note: Modified by the authors based on Hameide (2011)

and branding strategies, proposing alternatives to luxury for a better value. Premium brands have three sub-categories (Silverstein & Fiske, 2003):

- Super-premiums: priced at or near the top of their category such as Emporio Armani, these brands target consumers who belong to classes immediately below the traditional pure luxury customers.
- Old luxury brand extensions: lower-price versions of products created by companies such as Valentino Prêt-à-Porter whose brands have traditionally been affordable only by the rich.
- Masstige: priced well below super-premium or old luxury brand extensions such as Victoria Secret. It is oftentimes premium in terms of price and quality among mass products.

The critical success factor of the premium brand strategies lies in the prestige, differentiation, and a reasonable premium price. Companies need to invest resources to create a prestigious environment around the brand in order to promote public aspiration for the brand. Such an environment is created through availability in prestigious stores or sections in department stores, advertisement in glamorous magazines and fashion shows, and involvement of well-known designers. At the same time, adequate price premiums ensure limited access to the brand for the mass market. Ideally, middle-class consumers should have only occasional access to the brand (Truong, McColl & Kitchen, 2009).

The last brand category in Fig. 1.1 is mass-market brands. Products in these brands are generally mass-produced, widely distributed, and have a low selling price. The quality level of these products are acceptable (Hameide, 2011). The mass-market brand caters for a wide range of customers, producing ready-to-wear garments using trends set by famous names in fashion. In order to save money and time, they use cheaper fabrics and simpler techniques that can easily be produced by machines. Examples of mass-market brands are those found in mass retailers such as Tesco, Wal-Mart, Marks & Spencer, or specialty stores such as Old Navy.

Fashion brands can also be categorized by their distribution strategy as national or private label brands. Also called retail brands, private labels, and store brands (Herstein & Gamliel, 2006), these are brands of retailers—not producers and designers—who commission the production, market the products under their store name, and own the right to sell the brand exclusively in their retail outlets (Herstein, Gilboa & Gamliel, 2013). Examples include Club Room, INC, and Alfani, the private brands of American Macy's department store. Chain retailers such as Gap, Ann Taylor, H&M, Top Shop, Next, and Oviesse mainly sell their private brands only in their stores, and oftentimes, their brand and store names are the same (Hameide, 2011). The target of private brands ranges from mass market to premium brand, and retailers are increasingly developing more private labels for differentiation. In contrast, manufacturer brands are carried out by producers who have direct control over them. These brands are distributed in the national store chains, the reason they are also called national brands. Examples include Mexx, Guess, and Ralph Lauren.

Fashion Brand Development and Management

A brand is born when a name is given and copyrighted. Creation of a brand is a critical task for companies because the brand communicates their offering, values, and visions. In developing a brand, the most important decision is its positioning. This task can be accomplished by asking four questions: *what* is the benefit and purpose of the brand, *who* is the target potential customer, *what* are the differentiators that support and can create such a benefit, and *who* is the competition? This positioning process shapes the product mix and identity of the brand (Kapferer, 2012). Once a brand and its positioning is established, a firm needs to communicate the brand to its customers, which will be described in the next section. As a firm grows, a brand alone may not be enough to address the customers' diverse needs and increase market share. As such, many firms choose to extend its original brand. The following section focuses on two important decisions in brand growth: brand extension and brand portfolio strategy.

Brand Extension

Brand extension, the use of an established brand name to introduce a new product or class (Keller & Aaker, 1992), is one of the most highly utilized growth strategies in the fashion industry. Given that new product development requires high cost and its success is not high, brand extension is an economical option for fashion companies to increase their market share by leveraging the value of their existing brands (Aaker & Keller, 1990; Tauber, 1988). The brand that gives birth to a brand extension is termed the "parent brand." There are two types of brand extensions: horizontal (also called category extension) and vertical (or line extension) (Fig. 1.2). Brands extend horizontally to a new product class or category not currently offered by the brand but at the same price and quality level as the existing brand (Kim, Lavack & Smith, 2001). Examples of horizontal brand extension include Prada's introduction of fragrances and eyewear within the same price range and quality level as their parent brand. Brand can also extend vertically within the same product category either upward to target a more affluent market or downward toward more price-conscious consumers (Kim et al., 2001). In the fashion industry, vertical-downward extensions are more common than vertical-upward with many high-end fashion brands offering products at lower prices to capitalize on the value of their prestigious brand name (Kapferer & Bastien, 2009). Examples include Giorgio Armani's Emporio Armani and Armani Exchange, Calvin Klein's CK, and Donna Karen's DKNY and DK (Fig. 1.3).

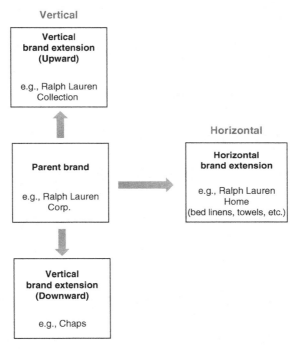

Fig. 1.2 Vertical and horizontal brand extension (*Note*: Developed by authors)

Ralph Lauren has sixteen levels of brands ranging from their highest-level runway brand, Ralph Lauren Collection, to the brand at the lowest price point, Chaps, which targets the mass market and price-conscious consumers (Ralph Lauren, 2013). Through brand extension, fashion firms reap numerous benefits—reducing the cost of developing a new brand including expense of introductory and follow-up marketing programs, increasing sales from additional consumer segments, and improving brand image and market coverages. However, the main issue with brand extension is the risk of diluting the parent brand image or confusing consumers (Aaker, 1991; Kim et al., 2001). Brand dilution will be further discussed under challenges and issues in luxury fashion branding in this chapter.

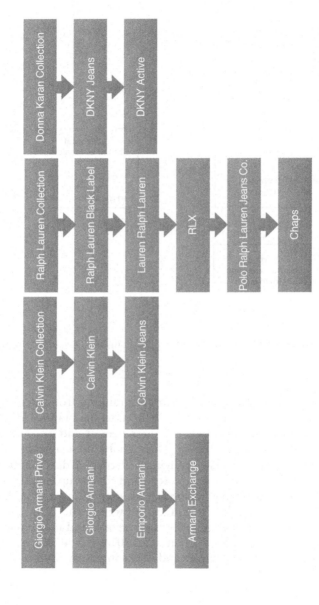

Fig. 1.3 Examples of vertical extension (*Note*: Developed by authors)

Brand Portfolio Strategy

In addition to brand extension, another way a company can grow is by creating new brands to meet the demands existing brands cannot satisfy. A company would thus carry multiple brands, or a "brand portfolio." A brand portfolio is defined as "a set of brands owned by one company" (Riezebos, 2003, p. 184) or "all the brands and their extensions, offered by a given company in a given product category" (Keller, 1998, p. 522). The decision about how to organize and manage a set of the brands is called a "brand portfolio strategy" or "multi-brand strategy." The term "brand architecture" describes the organization and structure of the brand portfolio, specifying brand roles and the relationship between brands and between different product-market contexts. Well-developed and managed brand architecture generates clarity, synergy, and brand leverage—three goals of brand architecture (Aaker & Joachimsthaler, 2002). The main question in a brand portfolio strategy is the relationship and domains among brands within the company. Failure to coordinate new brands with others in the portfolio can result in an incoherent combination. As such, companies must have a long-term vision for every brand in which roles and relationships among brands should be carefully defined (Keller, 1998).

Two main approaches exist in brand portfolio strategy: branded house and house of brands. A prominent example of a branded house is Armani. Each sub-brand is marked with the name Armani: Emporio Armani, Armani Casa, Armani Jeans, Armani Junior, Armani Caffé, Armani Fiori, Armani Hotel, etc. (Hameide, 2011) (Fig. 1.4). Hugo Boss serves as another example of branded house. Their brand portfolio includes five brands distinguished by colors. Boss in black logo offers the comprehensive spectrum of elegant business ensembles, casual sports clothing and evening wear. Boss Selection is another Boss brand in black color offering the premium tier. Orange color of Boss focuses on casual fashion while Green, on golf collection. The brand "Hugo" in red-colored logo offers men's and women's with unconventional and avant-garde fashion.

The branded house approach requires a minimum investment for each new brand because it leverages the status of an established name. This approach satisfies the three goals of brand architecture: clarity, synergy, and leverage. The advantages of this approach include effective increase of brand

Fig. 1.4 Armani Caffè, Armani Fiori (flowers), Armani Hotel and Ristorante (restaurant), Manzoni road, Milan, Italy (from the left) (*Note*: Photographed by Elena Cedrola, Milan, April 2016)

equity and enhanced marketing efficiency. A drawback to this approach is that if a brand within the portfolio falters, other brands suffer as well.

The other approach, house of brands, contains independent and unconnected brands. Oftentimes the corporate name is not evident, and as a result, consumers are unaware of the company to which the brand belongs (Aaker & Joachimsthaler, 2002). A prominent example of house of brands is the VF Corportation,[2] which owns and manages more than 30 brands. Major brands in their portfolio include North Face, Nautica, Lee, Wrangler, Timberland, Kipling, and Jansport. In this approach, association among brands can be avoided, thus establishing an independent brand image that focuses on specific markets. While this approach may be inefficient in marketing, it allows companies to avoid negative spillovers that may occur in the branded house approach.

Another example of a house of brands is LMVH, a French luxury conglomerate, which has more than fifty leading luxury brands in a number of market sectors such as fashion and leather goods, publishing and media, wines and spirits, and more (see Chapter 6 in this volume). Other leading luxury groups such as Kering, Prada, and Richemont also take the house of brand approach in the brand portfolio. As with VF Corporation, consumers are familiar with each brand but cannot easily connect the brands to their corporate group.

Fashion Brand Communication

Communication with target markets and with various shareholders plays a central role in developing and maintaining fashion brands. With the constantly expanding reach of the Internet and social media, an increasing number of global fashion houses utilize these tools for various purposes. After a brief overview of the use of traditional communication mixes such as advertising, celebrity endorsement, public relations and events, personal selling, storytelling and fashion tales in the fashion industry, this section will discuss the use of emerging media such as social media and blogs using notable examples.

Advertising

Advertising has always occupied a prominent place in the fashion industry's communication strategies. Print media has traditionally been favored by fashion companies, especially by luxury brands that rely on images.

The purpose of communication among luxury brands is not just to sell but also to inspire the consumer to identify with the brand. Specialized fashion magazines, such as Vogue, Elle, and GQ, employ this traditional tool to communicate brands and promote their images. This is why approximately 75 % of a fashion magazine constitutes of advertisements (Chevalier & Mazzalovo, 2008). However, with the advent of the digital era, the use of print media has been gradually declining (Glennie, 2015).

Fashion magazines have developed two noticeable innovations. In 1993, Salvatore Ferragamo was the first to introduce the gatefold—a cover page which can be folded over two or three times. This small change has allowed the Italian luxury brand to double their business ties over the previous year in the US market. Another innovation is the attachment of cosmetics or perfume samples in the magazine. This innovation has later expanded to attach accessories like bracelets for promotional purposes.

Billboards are another means of advertisements in the fashion industry. Though they resemble traditional media, billboards have recently become popular again thanks to technical innovations that have enhanced their quality. In comparison to the press, billboards are not more cost effective. Renting the scaffold at the Ducal Palace in Venice, for example, costs 40,000 Euros per month (Cappellari, 2011). Yet, despite this expense, billboards are effective because of the ability of images and written texts to evoke consumer associations—a more effective form of communication than radio, for example (Chevalier & Mazzalovo, 2008).

Celebrity Endorsement

Celebrities can help advertisements stand out (Erdogan, 1999) and enter new markets (Blecken, 2009) by attracting the attention of consumers. This technique creates positive associations with the brand and circulates the brand image. Nike, for example, has incorporated the image of basketball star Michael Jordan with its brand, making him an integral part their brand image. To use celebrity endorsement effectively, the image conveyed by the brand must be consistent with the selected character (Carroll, 2008).

Celebrity endorsement has become a common approach in many companies' branding strategies, especially among luxury brands. Gianni Versace, for example, relies on a group of models as endorsers. Today famous actors, pop stars, or prominent athletes replace the models. Some examples include Sofia Coppola for Marc Jacobs, Keira Knightley for Asprey, and Adam Brody for Ermenegildo Zegna.

Circulation of negative news on an endorser is a major risk of using celebrity endorsement, especially when the relationship has been consolidated over time (Till, 1998). An example is Kate Moss, the face of the perfume Coco Mademoiselle by Chanel in 2005 and endorser of H&M and Burberry. After a British tabloid caught her using cocaine, the brands she worked for rescinded their contracts. Beyond integrity, the brand must choose a character who shows a continued commitment to the brand over others. Otherwise, the public might consider the association as simply a business strategy, failing to associate the endorser with the brand (Passikoff, 2013).

Public Relations and Events

Public relations (PR) is defined as the planned and ongoing effort to establish and maintain goodwill and mutual understanding between an organization and the public (Blythe & Cedrola, 2013). PR aims to influence the perceptions that consumers have concerning a brand and build positive relationships between the company and its stakeholders. In the fashion and luxury industry, PR is an increasingly common and high-impact strategy that attracts media attention.

Events such as fashion shows and grand openings of stores are common PR tools used in the fashion industry (Chevalier & Mazzalovo, 2008). Fashion shows are important for both new designers and established brands. They primarily serve to inform the press and buyers of a brand's values, positioning, and products. In the mass market, fashion shows are organized internally to display new products to the staff and producers. In the luxury industry, fashion designers present their creations during the fashion weeks, targeting buyers and the international press (Jackson & Shaw, 2009). Fashion shows can also be used strategically to recover a brand's image. In 1997 when new CEO of Burberry, Rose Marie Bravo, was appointed, the company's profits dropped drastically. As a remedy, Burberry held Burberry Prorsum fashion shows in Milan twice a year, helping the company regain its positive image and increase sales (Moore & Birtwistle, 2004).

Opening a new store is another event that can be strategically designed to promote a brand. Burberry's decision to open a flagship store in New Bond Street in London, one of the most exclusive streets in the city, positioned Burberry next to numerous successful brands in the luxury sector such as Gucci, Versace, and Prada. Opening the store also increased coverage of the company in the mainstream media (Moore & Birtwistle, 2004).

Sponsorships are another category of events, an occasion when brands claim part of an event's identity (Chevalier & Mazzalovo, 2008). An example is the Grand Prix Hermès in Paris (http://www.sauthermes.com/en/), considered one of the most prestigious equestrian competitions internationally. The event has allowed Hermès to increase its association with competition, tradition, and aristocratic attitudes.

The last category of events consists of exclusive ceremonies, occasions in which the brand is linked to celebrities through events such as the Grammy Award MTV, the Oscars, and the Cannes Film Festival in France. A notable example is when Richard Gere wore Armani suits in the film "American Gigolo," evoking a prestigious image of the brand, which resulted in a steep increase in Armani sales after the film's release (Carroll, 2008).

Personal Selling

One of the most direct and traditional communications is through personal selling. In the luxury sector, products are often sold by the creator or specialists—people who are intimately familiar with its characteristics. In addition, this tool can be used to adapt products to consumers' needs through custom services. Through personal selling, companies obtain feedback from consumers, which can later influence product development (Okonkwo, 2007). As stated by Bernard Arnault, owner of LVMH Group, his brands sell dreams, not just products. As such, the person managing relationships with consumers must nurture this dream, giving customers the attention that she or he needs. The distance between salespeople and consumers vary by culture. In comparison to the West, the relationship between sellers and consumers in Asia are more distanced and hierarchical (Cedrola & Battaglia, 2012).

Storytelling and Fashion Tales

Many fashion companies create and implement their communication strategy within a broader, more integrated strategy built around a fashion tale. These narratives arise from the realization of a possible world—"a universe of meaning, or simply an imaginary, consisting of a specific set of values, settings, characters, symbols and patterns of action" (Ironico, 2014, p. 184). Four types of possible worlds are created in a fashion tale: likely, unlikely, impossible, and unthinkable. In the likely world, the narrative takes place in reality and does not require the alteration of physical laws. An example is the seasonal Fendi communication strategy, adopted in autumn/winter 2011–2012, which established the brand in the world of painting (Ironico, 2014). Chanel narratives belong to the possible world, creating a story around Gabrielle Chanel who, despite of her humble beginnings, succeeded in establishing a new style (Herskovitz & Crystal, 2010). The unlikely tales produce narratives in which the physical laws are partly altered. An example is the world created by the director of Mulberry during the London Fashion Week in February 2012 from the children's story *Where the Wild Things Are* by Maurice Sendak.

Fashion companies also adopt impossible or unthinkable worlds. An example is the advertisement created for the Fall and Winter fashion show of Alexander McQueen in 2012–2013 in which the leading model is a virtual entity composed of pixels, blending in with the psychedelic ambiance in the background. In this world, many physical laws do not line up with reality. Unthinkable scenarios are inspired by artistic vanguards, especially surrealism, and place subjects in unrealistic surroundings. With this strategy, it is possible to see soft watches, mustaches, lobster and bowler hats in unlikely places as often seen in Harvey Nichols shop windows, a luxury British clothing chain (Ironico, 2014).

Social Media

The spread of social media has also changed how fashion and luxury companies communicate. Social media are virtual applications that connect individuals by providing a platform for them to share content. The most prominent forms of social media include Facebook, Twitter, YouTube, Instagram, and MySpace. Facebook is predominantly used to launch new products (Indivik, 2011), build relationships with clients and fans (Touchette, Schanski & Lee, 2015), and create exclusive digital catwalks (Macchi, 2013). Twitter is a public relations tool, allowing companies to gauge consumer satisfaction through virtual chats. YouTube represents storytelling in the form of short films (Pace, 2008).[3] Examples on the uses of Facebook, Twitter, and YouTube are presented in Table 1.2.

Table 1.2   Selected examples of social media use in the fashion industry

Social media	Company/Brand	Activity
Facebook	Burberry	Allowed consumers to request of a free sample of a new perfume (Indivik, 2011)
	Oscar de la Renta	Launched a new perfume (http://wave.wave metrix.com/content/oscar-de-la-renta-launch-new-product-facebook-only-campaign-00747)
	Topshop	Provided digital catwalk
YouTube	Hermès	At Hermès YouTube channel, for example, the world of equitation is recounted through the video Voyage d'Hermès where Pegasus, the famous winged horse of Greek mythology, is revisited in a modern way. To communicate the craftsmanship a video traces the workday of its artisans (https://www.youtube.com/user/hermes).
	Fendi	Featured Whisperd project (videos that discover the traditional Italian know-how, describe the family tradition of the company and the brand's history from its origins) (https://www.youtube.com/watch?v=PnmM3Ul2NAI).
	Dior	Featured short films dedicated to the iconic bags (Macchi, 2013). A series of video that presents the fashion shows, the latest collections, and the network of partnerships that boasts the brand, Dior.
	Chanel	At Chanel YouTube channel, for example, short films telling the story of the brand or of a particular product and how to wear it properly; tutorials related to the make-up products are also provided (https://www.youtube.com/user/CHANEL).
Twitter	Donna Karan	Official account DKNY PR Girl (@dkny) that discloses to the brand followers everything that occurs behind the scenes (Macchi, 2013).
	Oscar de la Renta	Official account that discloses to the brand followers everything that occurs behind the scenes (Macchi, 2013).
	Kering Group	Twitter live chat #KeringLive created to discuss the issue of sustainability together with the Director of Sustainability Division.

Note: Developed by the authors.

Instagram is one of the best-known social applications for the fashion brands, allowing the brand to enhance its core values through images. That is why Burberry not only publishes photos related to its advertising campaigns but also images of characteristic corners in London. In doing so, the brand reinforces its heritage and the consumer's positive association with British culture. The Hermès approach is more focused on the product and its unique orange packaging. As such, it tends to share photographs focusing on its accessories (Macchi, 2013). Instagram also serves as a virtual platform where people can propose different styles and combinations using a hashtag (#). During the fashion show S/S 2014, Topshop invited his fans to post images with their favorite outfits and to comment on the fashion show using the hashtag #topshopwindow. These images were later published in special installations in the flagship store on Oxford Street in London.

In addition to the discussed forms of social media, other platforms such as Tumblr, Flickr, Pinterest, Foursquare, and eBay Fashion Gallery are also used. Moreover, fashion brands have increasingly developed smartphone applications—Chanel, Gucci, Ralph Lauren, Donna Karan being among them. In this way, the brand communicates its desire to create a lasting relationship with consumers (Kim & Ko, 2012).

Indeed, social media facilitate the development of integrated communication activities more easily and at a low cost. These platforms establish genuine, real-time relationships with consumers, allowing fashion labels to connect with the public in a way that an advertising budget previously would not allow (Prabhakar, 2010). In addition, social media greatly influence brand reputation—positive comments on a particular brand may impact consumers' purchasing behavior. Social media are also transforming public relations, enabling more engagement with the fashion public: "Traditionally, PR tactics focused on gaining media attention while marketing focused more on customer sales. However, social media has changed the playing field a bit, and PR is now concerned with more than just media and may be more involved in customer relationship building" (Noricks, 2012, p. 16).

Fashion Blogs

A fashion blog is an online space where fashion shows, new trends, fashion brands, designers' work, celebrity or personal style, tips, and product information are presented for people passionate about fashion

(Kulmala, Mesiranta & Tuominen, 2013). A fashion blog can be classified based on its author: blogs written by the industry's insiders and independent blogs. Insiders are those who have worked in the world of fashion or for traditional fashion media. Independent bloggers are fashion experts—frequent consumers whose opinions have significant weight on the choices of fashionistas.

Despite arising from the bottom, companies can no longer ignore the phenomenon of fashion blogs because their influence is comparable to famous journalistic sector headings (Cappellari, 2011). Stefano Gabbana, in an interview with Jessica Michault of International Herald Tribune, said: "Blogs are very important for us." Mr. Gabbana said. "We always keep them informed with our news and we always look them up because they represent a quick and spontaneous way to get fresh information." The rise of fashion blogs is evident when Dolce & Gabbana decided to seat famous bloggers in the front row of fashion shows, providing them with a computer to comment in real time. While designers previously had to wait at least a week for reviews on their new lines, they now receive immediate feedback because bloggers can comment in real time (http://www.nytimes.com/2009/11/17/fashion/17iht-rsocial.html).

Blogs are also source of free publicity for brand and stores, creating a name for emerging designers and adding prestige to established brands. For example, the fashion blog of 28-year-old Chiara Ferragni is one of the most viewed in the world. Her blog, "The Blonde Salad" (http://www.theblondesalad.com), is a virtual platform where Chiara daily publishes pictures, updates on her looks, adds comments about must-have's of each season, and advises her audience on clothing choices. The Milanese fashion blogger has earned more than 5.6 million followers on Instagram, 1.2 million on Facebook, and numerous collaborations with designers such as Christian Dior, Chanel, Louis Vuitton, and Max Mara.

CHALLENGES AND ISSUES IN LUXURY FASHION BRANDING

Companies face many challenges in managing brands. Luxury fashion brands experience more unique issues than mass-market brands because of their distinct characteristics. This section explains the four common challenges luxury fashion brands face: counterfeit goods, commoditization, brand dilution, and brand avoidance. This volume examines five cases to discuss these challenges and the strategies luxury fashion houses employ to overcome them.

Counterfeiting and Its Impact on the Luxury Sector

Counterfeiting is the violation of laws, regulations, and contractual obligations that protect the intellectual property rights of products. The development of technology has fueled the phenomenon of counterfeiting, allowing it to use the Internet to identify new products, simulate their authenticity, and quickly reach a large number of consumers.

The exponential growth of counterfeiting has resulted in the intervention of international organizations, national governments, and individual companies. The World Trade Organization (WTO) has issued an agreement on intellectual property rights related to trade (TRIPS), a contract to which all the members of the WTO are expected to adhere. In addition, other international conventions detail intellectual property rights and advise firms on how to protect these rights. These regulations are not treated with the same respect in the East and the West. Chapter 2 of this book describes the story of Italian premium brand Harmont & Blaine that underwent 10 years of legal disputes in China to resolve severe counterfeit problems.

Over the past decades, companies also have tried to counter the problem of counterfeiting by instigating repressive measures. Table 1.3 explains four anti-counterfeiting strategies: protection, collaboration, prosecution, and education (Cesareo & Pastore, 2014). Education is one of the most powerful weapons companies can employ to prevent counterfeiting and increase the awareness of stakeholders on the issue. Yet, according to statistics, a very high percentage of consumers consider counterfeiting in a positive light, as it allows them to buy products they otherwise could not afford (Kim & Karpova, 2010). Brands such as Rolex, Coach, and Ralph Lauren use their website to educate consumers and raise awareness of counterfeiting. The Rolex website, for example, contains an entire section devoted to the issue, listing strategies for consumers to distinguish an original product from its imitation.

Commoditization

A second challenge luxury brands face is the risk of their products being commoditized. The "commoditization" of a product is a process by which a good or service becomes widely available and interchangeable with goods or services provided by other companies. Commoditization is

Table 1.3 Anti-counterfeiting strategies

Strategies		Explanation
Protection	Tangible assets	Tangible assets can be protected using (i) Track-and-trace technologies to identify original products throughout the distribution channels, (ii) covert technologies (devices detectable by employees or surveillance agencies), and (iii) overt solutions (perceptible by customers)
	Intangible assets	Protection of intellectual properties (trademarks, patents, designs, models, and copyrights), and registration both nationally and internationally.
Collaboration	Safeguard of rights	Joint efforts with governments, judicial institutions, police forces, suppliers and distributors, auction websites and customs.
	Fight against counterfeiting on a global scale, lobbying power	Joint national and international intellectual property rights and anti-counterfeiting associations. Examples include WIPO (World Intellectual Property Organization), WCO (World Customs Organization), MARQUES Association of European Trademark Owners, INTA (International Trademark Association), IACC (International Anti-Counterfeiting Coalition), GACG (Global Anti-Counterfeiting Network), BASCAP (ICC) (Business Action to Stop Counterfeiting and Piracy) (International Chamber of Commerce).
Prosecution	Legal actions, administrative actions, raids and seizures and destruction of counterfeit goods	Against anyone who violates the rights: counterfeiters, auction websites, and discount department stores.
Education	Employees	Internal education to increase awareness and gain support.
	Suppliers Distributors	Clauses, agreements and reports of fakes travelling through the legitimate supply and distribution chains.
	Customs, Police forces	Information programs on the peculiarities and characteristics of authentic products.
	Consumers	Awareness and advertising campaigns on counterfeiting to obtain complicity.

Note: Developed by authors based on Cesareo and Pastore (2014)

caused by a series of actions such as deterioration, proliferation, and escalation (D'Aveni, 2010). Deterioration occurs "when firms develop strategies to reach the mass market from a position that was hitherto upscale" (Riot, Chamaret & Rigaud, 2013, p. 921). Proliferation describes companies' development of "new combinations of price-benefit products to attack traditional markets [...] as in the case of ready-to-wear collections." Escalation refers to competitors offering a similar product at a similar or lower price (Riot et al., 2013, p. 921). The commoditization trap affects all industries, but its effect on luxury industry can be detrimental because it shakes the industry's core tenets of luxury, rarity and exclusiveness (Dubois et al., 2001; Vigneron & Johnson, 1999, 2004). Luxury brands facilitate this process through brand extension to lower price points and by outsourcing its production to the low-wage countries.

To mitigate commoditization, many luxury brands communicate exclusivity and prestige by managing the use of art through arts sponsorships or philanthropic activities and creating limited collections in collaboration with artists. All these activities bind the luxury brand with the world of art and instill rarity. This art-based strategy is collectively referred to as "artification." Examples of "artification" include Louis Vuitton (detailed in Chapter 6), Gucci, and Valentino.

The Creative Director of Gucci, Alessandro Michele, started a collaboration with the NYC-based graffiti artist, Trouble Andrew. Andrew had been painting the city with the Gucci logo, yet instead of taking actions against him, Gucci's creative director decided to collaborate with him, transforming Andrew's graffiti into fashion prints. In "Ghost Gucci," the graffiti appeared in the collection in the form of decorate skirts, color bags, and embellished leather jackets. The fake became real—or rather, the real was contaminated, customized, and made unique. Valentino house has also created collections with artists such as Christi Belcourt (cues arising from the painting Water Song), Esther Stewart ("color block" aesthetics), Celia Birtwell (creation of precious fabrics with floral themes), and Giosetta Fioroni (introduction of the iconic romantic camouflage print) (http://www.valentino.com/it/shop/artisticcollaborationmain_section).

Following the luxury brands, some premium brands and private labels also began to collaborate with artists to enhance their value proposition. The American brand, Gap, has made t-shirts printed with an ink sensitive to UV rays, which changes after exposure to the sun. These prints reproduce the works of Alex Katz, Francois Berhoud, Yoko Ono, Roe Ethridge, Richiard Phillips, Ugo Rondinone, and Peter Lindbergh (http://becauselondon.com/fashion/2014/05/gap-tees.aspx).   This "artification" effort is evident when museums treat previous collections as art pieces. Ferragamo, for example, offers curated exhibitions with his personal history and previous collections in a corporate museum in Florence, Italy. More information can be found in Chapter 3 in this volume.

Brand Dilution

A third major challenge that luxury fashion brands experience is the risk of its brand image being diluted. Brand dilution occurs when "the favorable attribute beliefs consumers have learned to associate with the family brand name" are diminished (Loken & John, 1993, p. 79). In particular, this may occur when high-end brands extend downward to increase their market share. Brand extension is one of the most effective growth strategies, though if poorly managed it could dilute the distinctive image of the parent brand.

Probably the most well-known instance of brand dilution in the fashion industry is Pierre Cardin (Albrecht, Backhaus, Gurzki & Woisetchlager, 2013). Trained at the Christian Dior house in the 1940s, he was the first *haute couture* designer to launch a ready-to-wear collection, expand globally by opening stores all over the world, and license his name to a variety of products. Though he revolutionized the fashion business, his extensive use of licensing agreements for over 900 products ranging from fashion goods to hospital mattresses diluted his initial luxury brand image. When he expressed his intention sell his business empire, potential buyers were skeptical about the true value of his brand (Okonkwo, 2007). Pierre Cardin's experience illustrates that extended brands' increased availability and visibility among masses can harm the image of high-end parent brands (Kim et al., 2001) because one of the characteristics customers are attracted to luxury brands is their exclusivity (Escalas & Bettman, 2003). To avoid the adverse effect of brand dilution, many luxury houses like Gucci and Burberry bought back their licenses and re-positioned their brands to regain their luxury status (Okonkwo, 2007) by controlling their product availability to the masses. Indeed, one critical luxury branding strategy is maintaining its exclusivity, so any activity that makes luxury brands more available—either via licensing or brand extension—creates danger. To keep its exclusivity, a growing number of fashion brands limit their brand extensions through "limited edition" series, a concept that will be detailed under "trends in branding and communication in the fashion industry."

Brand Avoidance

Fashion houses consolidate a variety of values consumers seek in a brand. However, consumers at times deliberately reject a particular brand despite having the financial ability to access these brands. This is called "brand avoidance" (Lee, Motion & Conroy, 2009; Rindell, Strandvik & Wilén, 2013). Examples include anti-Starbucks (Thompson & Arsel, 2004) and anti-fast fashion movements (Kim, Choo & Yoon, 2013). Sustained periods of brand avoidance can create negative brand equity. As such, firms must respond in a timely manner to prevent avoidance or consider re-branding. Consumers actively reject certain brand for three reasons: unmet expectations, symbolic incongruity, and ideological incompatibility (i.e., moral avoidance) (Lee et al., 2009). That is, a consumer may choose not to purchase a brand again as a result of a negative experience (unmet expectation), a misalignment of a brand's symbolic imagery with the consumer's personality (symbolic incongruity), or disagreement with a brand's ethics such as the exploitation of a certain population in product development (ideological incompatibility) (Kim et al., 2013; Lee et al., 2009).

The rise of the Internet and social networking has allowed many consumers and online activists to spread their rejection of specific brands and raise awareness about unethical practices. In the luxury industry, items made from animal skin have rendered the sector a prime target by animal rights and environmental activists. Gucci, in particular, has been at the center of violent debates over the use of animal skins in its products. To recover from this negative image, Gucci was the one of the first luxury brands to sign a certification on corporate social responsibility and later donated 10 million dollars for the education of women and girls in developing countries. In a global campaign called Chime for Change in 2013, Gucci promoted the education of women in developing countries and justice and health services in cooperation with celebrities like Halle Barry and Jennifer Lopez (Doran, 2014). Hermès has also suffered from backlash from PETA's (People for the Ethical Treatment of Animals) campaign against the brand's exploitation of alligators in its production of handbags.

As such, depicting respect for the environment and human rights has become a way for brands to distinguish themselves from their competitors. Hugo Boss, for example, announced in a 2014 report that they have abandoned the use of animal fur in its collection. The brand also joined the international coalition Fur-Free-Alliance (FFA), an organization that unites 38 organizations for animal protection (Fur Free Alliance, 2015).

Trends in Branding and Communication in the Fashion Industry

With the plethora of communication through various social media platforms, fashion brands must find unique ways to capture consumers' attention and establish its values and images. This chapter introduces five prevalent trends fashion companies employ to expand its reach: luxury brand's offering online, limited edition, guerrilla marketing, pop-up stores, and reinforcing brand equity through experiential spaces. These five trends appear to be discrete; however, they are connected in their effort to capture a large market share (e.g., online selling) while creating pleasant and impactful surprises for consumers (e.g., limited edition, guerrilla marketing, pop-up stores), further reinforcing a brand's images by offering experiences outside their stores.

Luxury Brands' Offering Online

The impressive growth of online retailers, especially in the fashion sector, is well known. The clothes and sports goods sector alone constitutes the 60 % of online purchases in the European Union (Eurostat, 2015), and cross-border online shopping through American Amazon.com and UK Asos.com is growing exponentially (Jin & Cedrola, 2016). However, less known is the increasing number of luxury brands offering online sales. Previously, mass retailers in the industry have been leading online sales, and a majority of luxury brands have largely used their home pages as a promotional tool, not considering it to be a sales platform. According to McKinsey & Co., global digital sales for women's luxury fashion are expected to grow from a current 3 % to 17 % by 2018 with a total market size of $12 billion (Schmidt, Dörner, Berg, Schumacher & Bockholdt, 2015). Similarly, a recent market research report estimates that online sales could make up to 40 % of luxury sales by 2020 (Gustafson, 2016). In particular, China alone is expected to experience a 70 % growth in online luxury sales (Schmidt et al., 2015). The importance of online sales has prompted several luxury brands including Giorgio Armani and Valentino to shift from outsourcing their digital platform to keeping it in-house to maintain their online operations better. LVMH also recently hired a senior executive from Apple Inc. to direct the company's digital push (Roberts, 2015).

Leading examples of luxury brands that sell products directly from their corporate website include Burberry, Michael Kors, Prada, Hermès, and

Gucci. Burberry, in particular, began to sell online relatively early in 2006, and e-commerce now represents about 10 % of their sales (Roberts, 2015). For Michael Kors, e-commerce accounted for 7 % of North American sales in 2015 (Milnes, 2015). Tom Ford and Fendi have also joined this trend, starting their online sales in 2014 and 2015, respectively.

Further, an increasing number of luxury brands are also offering their products indirectly through websites of selected high-end department stores and online luxury specialty stores such as Net-A-Porter.com and LuisaViaRoma.com. Established in the United Kingdom in 2000, Net-A-Porter is one of the world's premier online luxury specialty stores and ships to more than 170 countries, offering a seamless shopping experience across mobile phones, tablets, and desktops. Relatedly, online luxury specialty stores selling off-season items are increasing in popularity, among which include Yoox.com (established in Italy in 2000) and theOutNet.com (established in the United Kingdom in 2009). Two leading online luxury retailers, Yoox and Net-A-Porter, formed Yoox Net-A-Porter Group in 2015, which features most leading luxury brands on one website (http://www.ynap.com/it/), similar to an offline department store that has sections of a variety of brands.

In addition to online sales, luxury brands such as Gucci, Louis Vuitton, Cartier, and Chanel have also begun offering an application for mobile phones. These online and mobile channels have allowed luxury brands to capture greater number of consumer groups—including those pressed for time and rural customers who do not access to local boutiques (Schmidt et al., 2015). One challenge of online luxury retailing is the risk of overexposure while maintaining its exclusivity (Okonkwo, 2009). To combat this challenge, luxury brands have strived to create well-designed sites, providing consumers with an exceptional digital experience.

Limited Edition

A growing trend in both designer brands and mass brands is the introduction of limited edition products by restricting the quantity produced and the amount of time it is available to consumers (Balachander & Stock, 2009). Limited edition became popular after H&M's successful collection with Karl Lagerfeld in 2004. Ever since, H&M has continued to create limited collections with many leading designers—such as Stella McCartney in 2005,

Jimmy Choo in 2009, and Versace in 2011 and 2012—and celebrities—
Madonna in 2007 and Beyoncé in 2013 (Childs & Jin, 2016). The popularity of limited edition is expanding to many different levels: mass brands
and leading designers (e.g., H&M), mass retailers and leading designers
(e.g., Target with Missoni), and luxury brands and leading artists (e.g.,
Louis Vuitton with Takashi Murakami and Yayoi Kusama). A successful
example of limited edition was "Missoni at Target," during which hundreds
of consumers lined up outside in anticipation and Target homepage was
crashed throughout the day due to high traffic (CBC News, 2011). The
Louis Vuitton's collaboration with Japanese artists Takashi Murakami and
Yayoi Kusama is detailed in Chapter 6.

Limited edition offers numerous benefits for involved parties and
consumers—exposing brands to mass markets, increasing sales, and pro-
tecting brand image from diluting at the same time (Childs, 2014). First,
limited edition is an effective way for both leading and rising designers to
circulate their brands to masses without losing their image by creating as
a test market for upcoming designers. It also provides an avenue for
high-end designers and brands to increase their exposure to mass markets, some of whom may become potential consumers in the future.
Second, it increases sales for both collaborators because limited offers
create a sense of urgency and exclusivity, discouraging consumers
from postponing their purchase (Balachander & Stock, 2009). Third, it
protects brands from diluting because the product has a limited availability (Berthon, Pitt, Parent & Berthon, 2009; Ginman, Lundell &
Turek, 2010). These benefits have prompted many leading US department stores such as Macy's and Kohl's to join this trend. Limited edition
has recently evolved to collaborate with other entities to strengthen its
image as well, including charity organizations to create a philanthropic
image. An example is Gucci's partnership with UNICEF, in which Gucci
released specially designed, limited edition handbags to represent the
collaboration. However, not every limited edition is a success, an example being the collaboration between Neiman Marcus, an upscale US
department store, and Target in 2013 (Childs & Jin, 2016).

Guerrilla Marketing

The saturation of communication tools in corporate marketing has pushed
many brand managers to adopt non-conventional forms of communication,
such as "guerrilla marketing" and "viral marketing" (Jackson & Shaw, 2009).

Coined, by Jay Levinson in 1982, the term guerrilla marketing indicates communication activities that surprise the audience, thereby imprinting the brand on the consumers' minds. It adopts both alternative communication channels and traditional media, and generally, its budget is limited (Dahlén, Granlund & Grenros, 2009). Examples of guerrilla actions are events that trigger a big buzz among consumers and gain visibility among mainstream media, though it occurs for a limited period of time (Ferrari, 2009). Guerrilla marketing also makes use of other means such as stickering,[4] ambush marketing,[5] viral marketing,[6] and flash mobs.[7]

Nike has successfully integrated the actions of guerrilla marketing in its communication strategy, using them as an alternate to traditional media. In July 2005, Nike celebrated the victory the NBA player Tony Parker by covering the Statue of Liberty in Paris with his official t-shirt. Though the shirt was removed by authorities, the act was seen around the world in minutes, increasing Nike's visibility. Only a month before this guerrilla action, Nike had exploited the phenomenon of circlemakers[8] to draw large footprints (campaign called BigFoot) in Rome and Milan, attracting the Italian media's attention (http://www.cmakers.org/nike.html).

Diesel is another brand that often adopts unconventional communication techniques. In 2007, the brand introduced the Heidies campaign (which is still ongoing) to promote the launch of a line of underwear in which two girls, the so-called Heidies, kidnapped a young man, Juan, detaining him in a hotel room for five days. The campaign quickly became viral because the company's site streamed it in real time and it required public interaction. In April 17, 2009, the company launched another campaign with the slogan "survive the crisis with Diesel Black Money" distributing black bills in 23 countries that gave customers a 30 % discount off of Diesel clothing. The Spanish brand Desigual opened the Kiss tour in Paris, London, Berlin, and Madrid in 2010, an event open to all who wanted to exchange a kiss. The kiss served as a symbol of affection that corresponds with the company's philosophy (think positive) to spread positive messages like a kiss, synonymous with love.

One of the most successful brands to create a viral campaign is Uniqlo. After a sales campaign in 2009 that inspired millions of people to line up in front of Uniqlo offline stores, the Japanese fashion retailer, seeking to boost its sales, launched the world's first online line waiting contest called The Lucky Line in 2010 to celebrate the brand's 26th anniversary. The online contest took place on the brand's website and allowed Twitter and Facebook users to join a virtual line by auto-tweeting their virtual line number. Each 26th user in the line was awarded with a thousand yen's worth of coupons to shop in Uniqlo stores. As a result, many people from all over the world lined up virtually in attempt to win the coupons. The campaign reached over 180 thousand people in Japan, 630 thousand in Taiwan, and 1.3 million in China, generating record sales of more than 10 billion yen in a single day in Japan. Moreover, The Uniqlo Lucky Line became the top trend on Twitter, helping Uniqlo win a Cannes Cyber Lion in 2011. Ultimately, guerrilla marketing relies on surprises to trigger an infectious buzz and maintain brand recall.

Pop-Up Stores

Pop-up stores are temporary shops that stay open for a limited period of time, usually from a week up to 1 year, and are located in various places including street corners, shopping centers, and airports (Pomodoro, 2013). Pop-up stores can be a form of guerrilla marketing because its appearance can surprise consumers. There are a variety of pop-up stores, ranging from modular retail establishments to those housed in shipping containers.

Pop-up stores have several advantages. The first is affordability because these stores are temporary and smaller in size than conventional retail stores, thereby reducing the cost of rent and the period of commitment. Moreover, a brand can open up a pop-up shop when high sales are expected and then close during the slower months. The low-cost and temporary nature of pop-up shops allow brands to test new products to gauge future demand. Another advantage is that pop-up retail establishments draw attention from crowds and create buzz around the brand, thus serving as a marketing tool (Pomodoro, 2013). People are interested in the sudden existence of a store, especially if it looks unique, like a shipping container for example. Lastly, these shops create a sense of urgency among consumers. Unlike traditional retail establishments, the pop-up store is presented as a "limited-edition" item, compelling people to take advantage in the moment.

Pop-up store has also several disadvantages. Competent temporary staff can be hard to find, and supervision can become an issue. Another problem is the technological investment required for the temporary shop. Although outfitting for a pop-up is minimal, these shops nonetheless require fixtures for merchandise and a point of sale area for transactions. Pop-up stores also risk damaging their brand image if they are not carefully maintained.

The first pop-up store was opened in 2004 by the Japanese brand Comme des Garçons, in an old bookshop in the Mitte district of Berlin. Though the neighborhood was isolated from the main fashion streets, posters around the city and a website communicated the brand. Following the lead of Comme des Garçons, several of fashion and luxury brands have integrated temporary shops into their communication strategy to increase brand awareness and strengthen their image. Chanel, for example, opened its first Nail Bar, a pop-up boutique, in the heart of London on July 24, 2012, to celebrate the opening of the Olympic Games. The store was distinguished by its industrial architecture, and inside, costumers could converse with make-up artists and stay up-to-date on the latest fashion trends. In addition, Chanel also opened a website entirely dedicated to the pop-up store. The case of Chanel illustrates an example in which temporary shops can provide an outlet for consumers to acquire a different experience with the brand and understand its values.

The two key strategies used by pop-up stores are location and time. Shop location should be surprising. As such, companies should take advantage of unusual places such as museums, desecrated churches, former warehouses, or other unconventional structures. Many industry brands have also chosen mobile locations such as buses or vans to allow the brand to reach many places. A remarkable example is the nomad pop-up store of Puma, built on three floors and featuring twenty-four containers.

The geographical area surrounding a pop-up can provide an advantageous element for the brand. An example is Soho, one of the trendiest neighborhoods in New York, which has become the prime location for brands such as Anna Sui, Gucci, Yohji Yamamoto, and Piperline. Another strategy used by pop-up stores is timing. Many brands open during a fashion week or during special occasions like Christmas. Chanel, for example, opened a pop-up store in Cannes in conjunction with the Film Festival.

Reinforcing Brand Equity by Offering Experiential Spaces

The final trend in the branding efforts of fashion houses is reinforcing its brand equity by offering experiential spaces. Pine and Gilmore introduced "experience economy" in a 1998 *Harvard Business Review* article, describing it as the next economy following the agrarian economy, the industrial economy, and the most recent service economy. They claimed that offering memorable experiences can become a product, like how the US Build-A-Bear Workshop[9] retailer charges their clients for a hosting a birthday parties. Incorporating experience into sales space has been observed in US retail chain Recreational Equipment, Inc. (commonly known as REI[10]) and Prada's three Epicenters in New York, LA, and Tokyo. REI offers rock climbing pinnacle inside of their flagship store in Seattle, United States and rock climbing lessons. Prada's use of Epicenter as part of their branding effort will be further discussed in Chapter 5 in this book.

Drawing on the concept of experiential retailing, defined as creating the brand experience for consumers (Sullivan & Heitmeyer, 2008), fashion brands have increasingly turned their flagship stores into experiential retail sites. Flagship stores are usually operated by manufacturers who have the intention of reinforcing their brand image because "consumers go to flagship brand stores not only to purchase products; they go to experience the brand, company, and products in an environment largely controlled by the manufacturer" (Kozinet et al., 2002, p. 18). Nike Town is a classic example of a flagship store offering an experience to its consumers. All five cases in this book depict how each European luxury and premium brand utilizes their flagship stores to develop and reinforce their brand image by offering a brand experience.

Leading luxury brands have been striving to provide more diverse experiences through hotels, restaurants, and cafés. Examples of landmark hotels by luxury brands include Bulgari hotel in Milan and Bali, Palazzo Versace in the Australian Gold Coast and Dubai, and Armani Hotel in Milan and Dubai. Further, Armani offers Nobu restaurant within Emporio Armani in Milan and Polo Ralph Lauren offers a restaurant within their flagship store in Chicago. French retailer L'Occitane en Provence operates L'Occitane Café in Taipei, Taiwan. Agnes B, French apparel and accessories retailer, has launched Agnes B Cafés in Hong Kong and Taipei. These hotels, restaurants, and cafés reinforce their brand image and create a more holistic vision for the brands. In doing so, atmosphere and architecture can be perfectly matched with brand image—such as Armani's modern sophistication and Bulgari's elegant contemporary. In these spaces, fashion brand logos are strategically placed on items such as room decorations, bed linen, towels, soap, plates, and silverware, further creating emotional attachment to the brands.

Brands evolve like human beings; once it is born, it should be nurtured for continued growth. As humans need constant interaction with others to build and maintain relationships, brands require similar attention. Brand creation is not an easy task. Sustaining growth requires well-orchestrated and integrated strategies guided by the corporate's long-term vision. This requires a fashion firm's vigilant and steady effort. This chapter reviews brand as a critical asset to fashion companies, highlighting the major concepts, challenges, and trends pertinent to fashion brands. The trends and challenges outlined in this chapter vary with changes in the environment. In contrast, brand image is the culmination of fashion houses' branding efforts. As such, if strategically managed, brand image will be enduring, bringing the company profits for years to come.

NOTES

1. Interbrand, a brand strategy agency, announces Best Global Brands report every year that identifies the 100 most valuable global brands based on financial results and projections in its own model for brand valuation. To qualify, brands must have (i) a presence on at least three major continents, (ii) must have broad geographic coverage in growing and emerging markets, (iii) Thirty percent of revenues must come from outside the home country, and (iv) no more than 50 % of revenues should come from any one continent (http://interbrand.com/best-brands/best-global-brands/2015/ranking/#?listFormat=ls)
2. Established in 1899, VF Corporation is a US company headquartered in Greensboro, North Carolina.
3. Intensive use of this media by many fashion brands led to the birth in 2012 of Fashiontube. On this channel, users can upload videos of famous fashion bloggers, fashion shows, and short movies related to the sector (Macchi, 2013).
4. The stickering consists of posting a number of stickers in busy areas so as to promote a brand already known or emerging.
5. The term ambush marketing refers to disruptive actions, carried out for example in a sponsored event, not conducted by the sponsor, but by a rival brand (Ferrari, 2009).
6. Viral marketing is a method of creating buzzwords or marketing pieces that are memorable and attention-grabbing. This method of marketing utilizes social media, videos, text messaging, and other person-to-person methods to spread information about a product or service instead of just creating a commercial and putting on TV or radio.

7. The term flash mob is used to indicate a group of people who plays short unconventional actions at a predefined location. The purpose of this action is generally ludic, but social or dissenting objectives cannot be excluded. People agree on the gathering place via SMS or Internet and their show is exhausted in a short time and ends with the applause of participants who vanish soon after (Ferrari, 2009).

8. Three decades ago, two men began flattening circles into the fields of Hampshire and Wiltshire. Little did they know that their Friday night antics would seed an international phenomenon that continues to change people's lives to this day (Irving, Lundberg & Pilkington, 2006).

9. Build-a-Bear Workshop is a US retailer that sells teddy bears and other stuffed animals. "Customers go through an interactive process in which the stuffed animal of their choice is assembled and customized during their visit to the store" (https://en.wikipedia.org/wiki/Build-A-Bear_Workshop)

10. REI is a US retail chain carrying gear, apparel, and footwear for a wide range of outdoor and fitness activities.

References

Aaker, D. (1991). *Managing brand equity; capitalizing on the value of a brand name*. New York: The Free Press.

Aaker, D. (1992). The value of brand equity. *Journal of Business Strategy, 13*(4), 27–32.

Aaker, D., & Joachimsthaler, E. (2002). *Brand leadership*. New York: Free Press.

Aaker, D. A., & Keller, K. L. (1990). Consumer evaluations of brand extensions. *Journal of Marketing, 54*(1), 27–41.

Albrecht, C. M., Backhaus, C., Gurzki, H., & Woisetchlager, D. M. (2013). Drivers of brand extension success: What really matters for luxury brands. *Psychology and Marketing, 30*(8), 647–659.

Balachander, S., & Stock, A. (2009). Limited edition products: when and when not to offer them. *Marketing Science, 28*(2), 336–355.

Berthon, P., Pitt, L., Parent, M., & Berthon, J. P. (2009). Brand, aesthetics and ephemerality: observing and preserving the luxury. *California Management Review, 52*(1), 45–66.

Blecken, D. (2009). Can overseas celebrities sell brands in China?. *Media: Asia's Media & Marketing Newspaper*, 16.

Blythe, J., & Cedrola E. (2013). *Fondamenti di marketing*. Milano-Torino: Pearson Italia.

Cappellari, R. (2011). *Marketing della moda e dei prodotti lifestyle*. Roma: Carocci Editore.

Carroll, A. (2008). Brand communications in fashion categories using celebrity endorsement. *Journal of Brand Management, 17*(2), 146–158.

CBC News. (2011). Missoni craze crashes Target website. Retrieved from http://www.cbcnews.com.

Cedrola, E., & Battaglia, L. (2012). *Storia, economia, cultura, modelli di business e di marketing per operare con successo in Cina. La via verso la terra di mezzo.* Milano: Cedam.

Cesareo, L., & Pastore, A. (2014). Acting on luxury counterfeiting. In B. Berghaus, G. Müller-Stewens, & S. Reinecke (Eds.), *The management of luxury: a practitioner's handbook* (pp. 341–359). London: Kogan Page.

Chevalier, M., & Mazzalovo, G. (2008). *Luxury brand management: una visione completa sull'identità e la gestione del settore del lusso.* Milano: Franco Angeli.

Childs, M. (2014). *Effective fashion brand extensions: the impact of limited edition and perceived fit on consumers' urgency to buy and brand dilution.* Unpublished doctoral dissertation. The University of North Carolina at Greensboro, U.S.A.

Childs, M., & Jin, B. (2016). A new age in apparel brand and retailer collaborations: trends and recommendations for a successful partnership. *Journal of Brand Strategy, 5*(1), 83–100.

Ciappei, C., & Surchi, M. (2011). *La mitopoiesi della marca moda: strategie di brand building nelle imprese moda.* Milano: Franco Angeli.

Dahlén, M., Granlund A., Grenros M. (2009). The consumer-perceived value of non-traditional media: effects of brand reputation, appropriateness and expense. *Journal of Consumer Marketing, 23*(3), 155–163.

D'Aveni, R. A. (2010). Beating the commodity trap: how to maximize your competitive position and increase your pricing power. *Harvard Business School Press Books.* Retrieved from http://search.ebscohost.com/login.aspx?direct=true&db=bth&AN=43454475&site=ehost-live; http://hbr.org/product/a/an/3153-HBK-ENG. doi:10.1225/3153

Doran, S. (2014, January 29). Gucci steps towards sustainability. *Luxury Society.* Retrieved from http://luxurysociety.com/articles/2014/01/gucci-steps-towards-sustainability

Dubois, B., Laurent, G., Czellar, S. (2001). Consumer rapport to luxury: analyzing complex and ambivalent attitudes. *Les Cahiers de Recherche, 33*(1), 1–56. Retrieved from http://www.hec.fr/var/fre/storage/original/application/5ecca063454eb4ef8227d08506a8673b.pdf

Erdogan, B. Z. (1999). Celebrity endorsement: a literature review. *Journal of Marketing Management, 15*, 291–314.

Escalas, J. E., & Bettman, J. R. (2003). You are what you eat: the influence of reference groups on consumers' connection to brand. *Journal of Consumer Psychology, 13*(3), 339–348.

Eurostat. (2015). Statistics explained. Retrieved from http://ec.europa.eu/eurostat/statistics-explained/index.php/E-commerce_statistics_for_individuals

Ferrari, F. (2009). *Marketing e comunicazione non convenzionale: guerrilla, virale, polisensoriale, emozionale.* Bologna: CLUEB.

Fur Free Alliance (2015). About us. Retrieved from http://www.furfreealliance.com/about-us/

Ginman, C., Lundell, C., & Turek, C. (2010). *Luxury for the masses: a study of the H&M luxury collaborations with focus on the images of the luxury designer brands.* Unpublished thesis. Uppsala University, Uppsala, Sweden.

Glennie, A. (2015, February 18). UK's digital advertising spend set to outstrip all other forms. *The Guardian.* Retrieved from http://www.theguardian.com/media/2015/feb/18/digital-advertising-spend-set-to-outstrip-all-other-forms

Gustafson, K. (2016). Sales here have escaped the luxury goods slowdown. *CNBC.* Retrieved from http://www.cnbc.com/2016/06/16/luxury-sales-slowdown-isnt-happening-online.html

Hameide, K. (2011). *Fashion branding unraveled.* New York: Fairchild.

Herskovitz, S., & Crystal, M. (2010). The essential brand persona: storytelling and branding. *Journal of Business Strategy, 31*(3), 21–28.

Herstein, R., Gilboa, S., & Gamliel, E. (2013). Private and national brand consumers' images of fashion stores. *Journal of Product & Brand Management, 22*(5/6), 331–341. doi: 10.1108/JPBM-03-2012-0110

Herstein, R., & Gamliel, E. (2006). The role of private branding in improving service quality. *Managing Service Quality: An International Journal, 16*(3), 306–319. doi: 10.1108/09604520610663516

Indivik, L. (2011, August 19). Burberry brings fragrance sampling campaign exclusively to Facebook. Retrieved from http://mashable.com/2011/08/19/burberry-body-facebook/#fp9odHDkssqV

Interbrand. (2015). Interbrand Rankings 2015. Retrieved from http://interbrand.com/best-brands/best-globalbrands/2015/ranking/#?listFormat=ls

Ironico, S. (2014). *Fashion management: mercati, consumatori, tendenze e strategie di marca nel settore moda.* Milano: Franco Angeli.

Irving, R., Lundberg, J., Pilkington, M. (2006). *The art, history & philosophy of crop circle making.* London: Strange Attractor Press.

Jackson, T., & Shaw, D. (2009). *Mastering fashion marketing.* New York: Palgrave Macmillan.

Jin, B., & Cedrola, E. (2016). Overview of fashion brand internationalization: theories and trends. In B. Jin & E. Cedrola (Eds.), *Fashion brand internationalization: opportunities and challenges* (pp. 1–30). New York: Palgrave Macmillan.

Kapferer, J. (2008). *The new strategic brand management: creating and sustaining brand equity long term.* London: Kogan-Page.

Kapferer, J. N. (1999). *Les marques, capital de l'entreprise: créer et développer des marques fortes.* Paris: Éditions d'organisation.

Kapferer, J. N. (2012). *The new strategic brand management: advanced insights & strategic thinking* (5th ed.). London: Kogan Page Limited.

Kapferer, J. N., & Bastien, V. (2009). The specificity of luxury management: turning marketing upside down. *Journal of Brand Management, 16*(5), 311–322.

Kapferer, J. N., & Bastien, V. (2010). *Luxury strategy: sovvertire le regole del marketing per costruire veri brand di lusso.* Milano: Franco Angeli.

Keller, K. L. (1998). *Strategic brand management: building, measuring and managing brand equity* (2nd edn). Upper Saddle River, NJ: Prentice-Hall.

Kim, A. J., & Ko, E. (2012). Do social media marketing activities enhance customer equity? An empirical study of luxury fashion brand. *Journal of Business Research, 65*(10), 1480–1486.

Kim, C. K., Lavack, A., & Smith, M. (2001). Consumer evaluation of vertical brand extensions and core brands. *Journal of Business Research, 52*(3), 211–222.

Kim, H., & Karpova, E. (2010). Consumer attitudes toward fashion counterfeits: application of the theory of planned behavior. *Clothing and Textile Research Journal, 28*(2), 79–94.

Kim, H., Choo, H. J., & Yoon, N. (2013). The motivational drivers of fast fashion avoidance. *Journal of Fashion Marketing and Management, 17*(2), 243–260.

Kozinets, R. V., Sherry, J. F., Deberry-Spence, B., Duhachek, A., Nuttavuthisit, K., & Storm, D. (2002). Themed flagship brand stores in the new millennium: Theory, practice, prospects. *Journal of Retailing, 78*(1), 17–29. doi:10.1016/S0022-4359(01)00063-X

Kulmala, M., Mesiranta, N., & Tuominen, P. (2013). Organic and amplified eWOM in consumer fashion blogs. *Journal of Fashion Marketing and Management, 17*(1), 20–37.

Kumar, N., & Steenkamp, J.-B. E.M. (2013). *Brand breakout how emerging brands will go global.* New York: Palgrave Macmillan.

Lee, M.S.W., Motion, J., & Conroy, D. (2009). Anti-consumption and brand avoidance. *Journal of Business Research, 62*(2), 169–180. doi:10.1016/j.jbusres.2008.01.024

Loken, B., & John, D. R. (1993). Diluting brand beliefs: When do brand extensions have a negative impact? *Journal of Marketing, 57*(3), 71–84.

Macchi, J. (2013). *Lusso 2.0: nuovi paradigmi della comunicazione dei marchi di alta gamma.* Milano: Lupetti Editore.

Milnes, H. (2015). How 3 high-end brands balance luxury with e-commerce. *Digiday.* Retrieved from http://digiday.com/brands/3-high-end-brands-balance-luxury-e-commerce/

Moore, C. M., & Birtwistle, G. (2004). The Burberry business model: creating an international luxury fashion brand. *International Journal of Retail and Distribution Management, 32*(8), 412–422.

National Retail Federation. (2016). 2016 top 250 global powers of retailing. Retrieved from https://nrf.com/news/2016-top-250-global-powers-of-retailing#globaloutlook

Noricks, C. (2012). *Ready to launch: the PR Couture guide to breaking into fashion PR*. Charleston, SC: CreateSpace.

Okonkwo, U. (2007). *Luxury fashion branding: trends, tactics, techniques*. New York: Palgrave Macmillan.

Okonkwo, U. (2009). Sustaining the luxury brand on the Internet. *Journal of Brand Management, 16*(5), 302–310. doi:10.1057/bm.2009.2

Pace S. (2008). YouTube: an opportunity for consumer narrative analysis?. *Qualitative Market Research: An International Journal, 11*(2), 213–226.

Passikoff, R. (2013, December 12). When it comes to Nike celebrity endorsements, they have to make sure the shoe fits (LeBron). *Forbes*. Retrieved from http://www.forbes.com/sites/robertpassikoff/2013/12/12/if-the-nike-brand-dont-fit-lebron-cannot-commit-2/

Pine, B. J. II., & Gilmore, J. (1998). Welcome to the experience economy. *Harvard Business Review, 76*(4), 97–105.

Pomodoro, S. (2013). Temporary retail in fashion system: an explorative study. *Journal of Fashion Marketing and Management, 17*(3), 341–345.

Prabhakar, H. (2010). How the fashion industry is embracing social media. *Mashable*. Retrieved from http://mashable.com/2010/02/13/fashion_industry-social-media/

Ralph Lauren. (2013). About Ralph Lauren. Retrieved from http://www.global.ralphlauren.com

Riezebos, R. (2003). *Brand management: a theoretical and practical approach*. Harlow: Prentice Hall.

Rindell, A., Strandvik, T., & Wilén, K. (2013). Ethical consumers brand avoidance. *Journal of Product and brand management, 22*(7), 484–490.

Riot, E., Chamaret, C., & Rigaud, E. (2013). Murakami on the bag: Louis Vuitton's decommoditization strategy. *International Journal of Retail & Distribution Management, 41*(11/12), 919–939. doi:10.1108/IJRDM-01-2013-0010

Roberts, A. (2015). Luxury web battle looms as LVMH, Hugo Boss develop e-commerce. *Bloomberg*. Retrieved from http://www.bloomberg.com/news/articles/2015-10-05/luxury-web-battle-looms-as-lvmh-hugo-boss-develop-e-commerce

Schmidt, J., Dörner, K., Berg, A., Schumacher, T., & Bockholdt, K. (2015). The opportunity in online luxury fashion sales are rising, but what do consumers expect from a luxury digital experience? *McKinsey & Company*. Retrieved from https://www.mckinseyonmarketingandsales.com/sites/default/files/pdf/CSI_Online%20luxury%20fashion.pdf

Silverstein, M. J., & Fiske, N. (2003). *Trading up: the new American luxury*. New York: Portfolio Penguin Group.

Sullivan, P., & Heitmeyer, J. (2008). Looking at Gen Y shopping preferences and intentions: exploring the role of experience and apparel involvement. *International Journal of Consumer Studies, 32*(3), 285–295.

Tauber, E. M. (1988). Brand leverage: Strategy for growth in a cost-control world. *Journal of Advertising Research, 28*(4), 26–30.

Thompson, C.J., & Arsel, Z. (2004). The Starbucks brandscape and consumers' (anticorporate) experiences of glocalization. *Journal of Consumer Research, 31*(3), 631–642. doi:10.1086/425098

Till, B. D. (1998). Using celebrity endorsement effectively: lessons from associative learning. *Journal of Product and Brand Management, 7*(5), 400–409.

Touchette, B., Schanski, M., & Lee. S.E. (2015). Apparel brands' use of Facebook: an exploratory content analysis of branded entertainment. *Journal of Fashion Marketing and Management, 19*(2), 107–119.

Truong, Y., McColl, R., & Kitchen, P. J. (2009). New luxury brand positioning and the emergence of masstige brands. *Brand Management, 16*(5/6), 375–382.

Vigneron, F., & Johnson, L. W. (1999). Review and a conceptual framework of prestige-seeking consumer behavior. *Academy of Marketing Science Review, 1*, 1–15. Retrieved from http://www.amsreview.org/articles/vigneron01-1999.pdf

Vigneron, F., & Johnson, L. W. (2004). Measuring perceptions of brand luxury. *Brand Management, 11*(6), 484–506. doi:10.2466/pms.1991.72.1.329

Byoungho Jin is Putman and Hayes distinguished professor in the Department of Consumer, Apparel and Retail Studies at the University of North Carolina, Greensboro, USA. Dr. Jin's research area focuses on international apparel retailing and branding. She has published more than 100 refereed journal papers in top level journals and made 110 refereed presentations, published three books, four book chapters and 70 trade articles for the practitioner audience. She serves as an associate editor for *Clothing & Textiles Research Journal* and *Fashion & Textiles* and is on the advisory board of Korea Chamber of Commerce and Industry. She was a visiting scholar at King Saud University, Saudi Arabia in 2015–2016 and the University of Macerata, Italy in 2016.

Elena Cedrola is associate professor at the University of Macerata, Italy, where she teaches Management and International Marketing. She is also professor of International Marketing at the Catholic University of Milan. Italy. She was a visiting Scholar at the Beijing Normal University (China) in 2014–2017, and at the Paris IV Sorbonne University (France) in 2014–2015. Dr. Cedrola's research areas are international management and marketing for small and medium sized enterprises. She has an extensive portfolio of intellectual contributions comprising of refereed journal publications, presentations, invited keynote speeches, lectures and workshops. Her latest research focuses on country of origin in the industrial sectors.

CHAPTER 2

Harmont & Blaine: A Successful Dachshund to Build the Values and Brand Identity

Maria Colurcio and Monia Melia

Abstract Harmont & Blaine is one of the most dynamic and successful companies in the Italian fashion industry, with about 100 mono-brand stores throughout the world. Born as a small family business in Caivano, a small city in the Naples province, the company has achieved successful competitive performance in less than 10 years despite competing with international fashion giants. The brand enjoys international recognition as being synonymous with top quality casualwear. The company's philosophy reinterprets the Italian sartorial tradition through creative combinations of different colors, fibers, and patterns, in order to offer a high quality *total look* solution to its customers. Over the years, Harmont & Blaine has invested various resources in the building of a brand identity consistent with this philosophy. This case explains how the building of a strong brand identity requires the management of visual identity, brand promise, brand personality, and brand communication.

Keywords Brand promise · Brand personality · Brand communication · Made in Italy · Retailing

M. Colurcio (✉) · M. Melia
Department of Legal, Historical, Economic and Social Sciences,
University of Catanzaro, Catanzaro, Italy

© The Author(s) 2017
B. Jin, E. Cedrola (eds.), *Fashion Branding and Communication*,
Palgrave Studies in Practice: Global Fashion Brand Management,
DOI 10.1057/978-1-137-52343-3_2

Introduction

Established in 1993 by an Italian glove manufacturer, Harmont & Blaine (H&B) is an Italian sportswear brand recognized and appreciated all over the world, with 100 exclusive boutiques spanning 50 countries across five continents. The brand, visually depicted by a small dachshund, evokes images of a casual luxurious lifestyle characterized by a marked unconventional personality, particularly through its *Made in Italy* label. It expresses the company's continuous search for originality and innovation since its birth at the beginning of the 1990s, at a time when the Italian fashion house Giorgio Armani was promoting fashionable trends based on black and white colors. However, H&B made a breakthrough by introducing vivid colors such as blue, yellow, and red in the production of luxury casualwear clothes, as well as patterns such as stripes, flowers, or butterflies and fibers such as silk, cotton, wool, and leather. Such styles were unconceivable at that time for male consumers, except for certain items of beachwear.

The success of the brand over time has depended mainly on the combination of these choices with a *Made in Italy* strategy and with a Mediterranean style that allows the construction of a strong product identity. The H&B brand highlights a complex product concept that offers a trendy style and guarantees the quality of Italian sartorial craftsmanship. "The idea behind all Harmont & Blaine products is the *leisurewear*, that is, the synthesis of usefulness and chic attributes. They are expression of elegance and quality of the manufacturing, and shine respect to the competitors' products such as Ralph Lauren, since they offer creative details and excellent craftsmanship of the finishing" (Interview with Domenico Menniti, 2015).

H&B provides a "total look," offering shoes and accessories that complement an already well-assorted clothing product portfolio. Nevertheless, the shirt remains the queen of the collections, as it was the product primarily responsible for increasing the brand's reputation. Indeed, the H&B shirt conveys the product concept of the brand by combining its distinctive creative design (yarns, colors, patterns, fibers) with the sartorial tradition belonging to the shirt of the Neapolitan school,[1] which differs in terms of the high number of stitching and handmade embroideries. The use of another Neapolitan technique for handmade tailored jackets results in a typical fold at the shoulder, allowing for superior softness and comfort. Furthermore, some efforts toward innovation address the enhancement of product performance. For instance, an innovative active sweater has been manufactured using a special patented yarn that releases a lavender scent when worn.

In little more than two decades, H&B has achieved significant market goals and excellent performance. The company was awarded the Dun & Bradstreet "Rating 1—Index of Highest Reliability"[2] for extraordinary performances in financial management, both in 2008 and 2011. Its brand strategy can be examined as an evolutionary path. The first stage of brand management lasted several years: it focused on the building of visual identity through the choice of a logo and its colors (the blue dachshund). The second stage, until the end of the 1990s, identified the refining of the brand promise: the company improved the definition of its features and refined the attributes of its brand identity. The third stage, up to 2010, infused emotional characteristics into the brand to strengthen the brand's personality. The fourth stage, still in progress, is characterized by brand extension: Harmont & Blaine cafés have opened in Europe, women's and children's collections have been launched, and accessories lines have been added.

This case study explains how the building of a strong brand identity can support small manufacturing businesses when approaching the international market and when coping with global competitors. This chapter illustrates H&B's history, business activities, and branding and communication strategies since its birth. It concludes with a discussion about implications for both researchers and managers. This case was written using both primary and secondary data. Primary data comes from two interviews with H&B's CEO, Domenico Menniti (September, 2015; January, 2016); one interview with Marco Montefusco (AGB Company Spa Marketing Director[3]); visits to the H&B headquarters in Naples; and stores visits in Italy and Europe. Secondary data was gathered from trade, academic journals, and newspapers, as well as from company documents such as annual reports, annual financial statements, industry research, corporate websites, and social media.

COMPANY OVERVIEW

With its headquarters in Caivano, a small city in the Naples province, H&B is an international group comprising Harmont & Blaine SPA (the holding company) and its subsidiaries—Harmont & Blaine Switzerland (founded in 2010) and Harmont & Blaine France (founded in 2015).[4] The company was founded in 1986 as PDM for gloves manufacturing; in 1993, with the registration of the brand Harmont & Blaine, it changed its name and type of production to focus on the production of shirts. It currently employs more than 500 workers.

H&B's offering consists of an innovative and casual-wear look for men, women, and children, conveying elegance through a combination of *Made in Italy* quality with some creative details. H&B apparel targets dynamic people who prefer informal clothing and enjoy novelties. Its products provide an innovative mix of shapes, colors, patterns, and clothes, evoking the Italian sartorial traditional: "*We aim to satisfy the customer's needs, more and more exacting in the search for a specific style, distinguishing us from our competitors, for creativity, innovation, and quality*" (Interview with Domenico Menniti, 2015).

The H&B portfolio consists of men's, women's, and baby/junior lines with four brand names. H&B is characterized by its high quality and high price. Its benchmark is Ralph Lauren. Harmont & Blaine Jeans is a basic collection mainly sold through online boutiques, allowing for lower price and originality. Harmont & Blaine Sport is for outlet collections and does not display the dachshund logo. Harmont & Blaine Junior is the kids' collection (Table 2.1). In terms of product portfolio, men's shirts constitute 28 % of their business, followed by men's t-shirts at 25 %, men's slacks at 15 %, women's clothing at 18 %, and baby/junior clothing at 4 % (Harmont & Blaine, 2015b).

H&B's production is 100 % *Made in Italy;* 93 % is outsourced to selected Italian artisanal workshops and 7 % is made in-house, including certain stages of cutting, assembly and finish. Men's and women's products are realized by

Table 2.1 Brand Portfolio of Harmont & Blaine

Target	Product lines and categories	Brand
Men (20–45 years)	Clothing (shirts, polo, sweatshirts, coats, slacks, jackets, T-shirts)	H&B
		H&B Jeans
	Shoes and accessories (shoes, belts, scarves, hats, bags, leather goods, gloves, socks)	H&B Sport
	H&B Jeans (hats, scarves, belts, T-shirt)	
Women (20–45 years)	Clothing (shirts, polo, T-shirts, coats, jackets, slacks, dresses, skirts)	H&B
	Shoes and accessories (shoes, belts, scarves, gloves, hats, bags, leather goods)	
Baby (1–12 months) Junior (2 months to 16 years)	Baby (blankets, sheets, peluches, hats, rompers) Junior (shirts, polo, coats, slacks, T-shirts, accessories, belts, dresses)	H&B Junior

Note: Authors based on trade publications and corporate website

subcontractors, which are exclusively located in the Campania region (Interview with Domenico Menniti, 2015). This outsourcing is deployed through a collaborative relationship that allows H&B to control the quality of the products and the entire production process. Subcontractors are selected and trained by the H&B production staff and belong to a list of accredited partners that is updated every 2 years on the basis of company inspections and quality control reports. The relationship between company and craftsmen can be defined as a partnership: they share a common goal (high-quality production according to the Neapolitan sartorial tradition), collaborate to achieve that goal, and subsequently extract value from such a relationship. Awards are planned for artisans depending on the performance achieved by H&B every year. This strategically promotes the maintenance of quality attributes regarding *Made in Italy* with which H&B brand identifies. Indeed, Campania[5] is very important for the Italian fashion system, being renowned for the sartorial tradition and for subcontractors that work for large companies and internationally successful brands, such as Marinella[6] and Kiton.[7] Selected subcontractors also produce accessories and junior products. Specifically, "Harmont & Blaine shoes are realized with great care by a third-generation artisan company located in the heart of the Marche region, famous for shoes district in Italy. Indeed, the quality of the manufacturing and the craftsmanship of the finishing are the distinguishing elements of this entirely Made in Italy product" (Harmont & Blaine Facebook, 2015). The junior line is produced by AGB Company through an exclusive subcontractor agreement.

The Harmont & Blaine brand has developed a successful marketing strategy based on four pillars (Harmont & Blaine website, 2015): (a) Extension of the range and business lines, (b) Penetration of new markets, (c) Development of direct and indirect retail channels, and (d) Focus on direct dialogue with customers.

The extension of the range and lines has been a step-by-step process that drives the evolution of H&B's offering. Paying respect to the early stages of man shirt production, today the brand pursues a "total look" strategy offering new product categories (i.e., shoes and accessories) for new targets (women and 0–16-year-old children). As shown in Fig. 2.1, H&B has addressed new targets by adding "Harmont & Blaine Junior" in 2005, "Harmont & Blaine Sport" in 2010, and "Harmont & Blaine Jeans" in 2012. New categories were added by launching two "Harmont & Blaine Cafès" in 2009. The first is located in Porto Rotondo, one of the most exclusive and chic places of Sardinia, a well-known Italian luxury tourism destination (Fig. 2.2); the

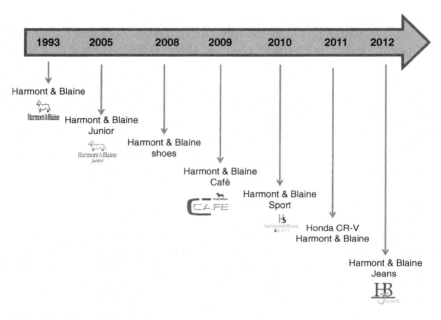

Fig. 2.1 Harmont & Blaine extension of the range and business lines (*Note*: Developed by authors based on trade publications and corporate website)

second can be found in Eboli, Campania, the region of the company headquarters. The Harmont & Blaine Cafés allow for total immersion for consumers into the lifestyle that the company has always sought.[8]

The second pillar, the penetration of new markets, refers to the beginning of the internationalization process that started in 2001. Although Italy remains its premier market, H&B sells its products throughout Europe, Africa, Asia, the Americas, and Oceania (Table 2.2). Indeed, since the early twenty-first century, the founders aspired to transform the brand from a local business into a global company. Through the "Global Cities" project, the company has penetrated the world's tourism and shopping capitals as strategic points for its worldwide development and visibility[9] (Fig. 2.3).

The third pillar comprises distribution through both direct (retail and e-commerce) and indirect retail channels (wholesale) (Table 2.3). The direct retail channel contributes 55.2 % to net sales (Harmont & Blaine, 2015a), including the exclusive boutiques (mono-brand stores), flagship stores, shops-in-shops, and factory outlets. The mono-brand stores, located

Fig. 2.2 Harmont & Blaine Café of Porto Rotondo, Italy (*Note*: Harmont & Blaine website)

in city centers or prominent international airports, are the main sources of influence for brand image. These stores are conceived as effective relational and experiential places (Melia, Colurcio, & Caridà, 2014), nurturing relationships with consumers and allowing their engagement in the

Table 2.2   International market penetration by Harmont & Blaine

Continents	Countries
Europe	Austria, Czech Republic, France, Germany, Italy, Malta, Republic of San Marino, Romania, Spain, Turkey, Ukraine, Cipro, Belarus
Africa	Albania, Algeria, Egypt, Morocco, South Africa, Tunisia, Congo
Asia	Armenia, Azerbaijan, China, Japan, Iraq, Lebanon, Kazakhstan, Kuwait, Saudi Arabia, Turkey, United Arab Emirates, Qatar, Uzbekistan, Russia, Singapore, Thailand, Malaysia, Jordan, Israel, South Korea, Georgia
America	Colombia, Dominican Republic, Mexico, Venezuela, Panama, United States
Oceania	Australia

Note: Authors based on corporate website

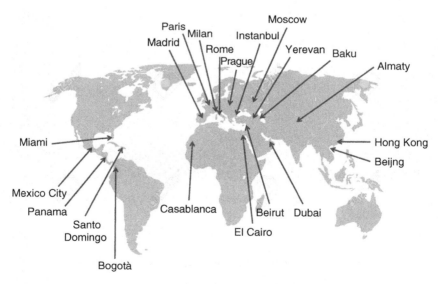

Fig. 2.3   Harmont & Blaine's presence in major global cities (*Note*: Developed by authors based on Harmont & Blaine website)

Table 2.3 Distribution network of Harmont & Blaine

Distribution channel	Type of store	Number	Location	Main cities and countries—partner
Retail	Exclusive boutiques	42	Italy	Turin, Naples, Rome, Milan, Florence, Palermo, Genova
		58	World	Yerevan (Armenia), Baku (Azerbaijan), Bogotá (Colombia), Santo Domingo (Dominican Republic), Cannes and Paris (France), Casablanca (Morocco), Mexico city (Mexico), Moscow (Russia), Madrid (Spain), Miami (United States)
	Shops in shopping mall	5	Italy	Catanzaro, Bergamo, Forlì-Cesena, Chieti, Mantova
		19	World	Almaty (Kazakhstan), Bucharest (Romania), Beijing (China), Santo Domingo (Dominican Republic), Almaty (Kazakistan), Dubai (United Arab Emirates), Doha (Qatar), Istanbul (Turkey), Panama City (Panama), Miami (United States); Beirut (Lebanon), El Cairo (Egypt), Bogotá (Colombia)
	Flagship stores	1	Italy	Milan
		3	World	Prague, Madrid, Moscow
	Outlets	22	Italy	

(continued)

Table 2.3 (continued)

Distribution channel	Type of store	Number	Location	Main cities and countries—partner
Wholesale	"Corner" within department stores or luxury Hotels	1	Italy	La Rinascente
		10	World	Galeries Lafayette (Dubai in United Arab Emirates), Sogo (Hong Kong in China), Casa del Estanco and Le Collezioni (Cartagena in Colombia), Palacio de Hierro (Mexico City in Mexico), El Corte Ingles (Madrid in Spain), Harry&Sons Werner Schuller (Wien in Austria), The Venetian Hotel (Macau in China).
	Multi-brand stores	About 600	Italy	Milan, Pavia, Turin, Rome, Agrigento, Palermo, Messina, Reggio Calabria, Catania
		About 200	World	Albania, Algeria, Armenia, China, Egypt, Germany, Iraq, Panama, Saudi Arabia, South Africa, Spain, Turkey, Ukraine, Uzbekistan.
e-commerce	Virtual Boutique	1		

Note: Authors based on corporate website

Harmont & Blaine "total look" experience. They are elegant places enhancing the Mediterranean roots of the brand without overlooking the local context. All H&B mono-brand stores reflect the Mediterranean blue and white color schemes that recall houses in Capri and Ischia, wood furniture inspired by Sardinia, and ceramics fulfilled in Vietri, in the province of Salerno near Naples (Fig. 2.4). Moreover, the mono-brand stores in international markets highlight the link between Italy and the host country.[10]

Fig. 2.4 Harmont & Blaine boutiques (*Note*: Harmont & Blaine website)

| Flagship store of Milan | Flagship store of Madrid | Flagship store of Prague |

Fig. 2.5 Harmont & Blaine flagship stores in Milan, Madrid, and Prague (*Note*: Harmont & Blaine website)

The flagship stores develop and reinforce market relationships and enhance business in international markets. From 2010 to the present, the company has opened four flagship stores in traditional fashion cities such as Madrid and Milan, as well as "emerging" cities such as Prague and Moscow. The H&B flagship stores enjoy prestigious spaces on the main fashion avenues, which facilitates advertising for all dachshund collections, footwear, and accessories, as well as entertainment elements. They offer large and well-lit environments of about 530 square meters in Milan and Madrid, designed with colors and materials that recall the Mediterranean essence and represent a "lifestyle store." The Prague flagship store is the largest of all H&B flagship stores in the world. Developed on four levels in the city center, the new store covers over 1,000 square meters of the historical Palace of the Golden Lira "Zlatá Lyra," a building protected by cultural heritage and characterized by a precious wooden facade with gold decorations (Fig. 2.5).

Shops-in-shops depend on an agreement with department stores to rent retail space where H&B runs another independent store. This type of arrangement is becoming increasingly popular among high fashion brands such as Ralph Lauren, Calvin Klein, and Armani. H&B already holds an agreement with well-known American department stores. During the last 5 years, the company has opened many "shops in shops" in Turkey, United States, China, the Dominican Republic, Kazakhstan, Panama, Egypt, and Colombia, where the cheaper Harmont & Blaine Jeans collection is sold.

Recent factory outlets and shops-in-shops have followed the general trend of fashion distribution and mirror the behaviour of the main competitor.

"*From 2010, there isn't a prestigious and luxury brand or a fashion giant that is not present in some outlets. Well-known brands such as Valentino, Prada, Ferragamo, Gucci, Tod's, Ralph Lauren, Dolce and Gabbana, Burberry, Hugo Boss, Max Mara, Tommy Hilfiger, Brooks Brothers, Tom Tailor and others find the outlets an additional channel for their product offerings*" (Interview with Domenico Menniti, 2015). The company has opened 22 factory outlet stores where consumers can find products discounted by 35 %.[11] The e-commerce channel is recent, but its performance is flourishing. "Shop.harmontblaine.it" is a new direct way for the company to deal the dachshund products and reinforce its relationships with consumers; it yielded €972,000 of revenue in 2014 (Interview with Domenico Menniti, 2015).

H&B's indirect channels include multi-brand stores and "corners." Multi-brand boutiques contribute to cover key markets especially in Europe (Spain, Romania, Ukraine), the Middle East (Lebanon, Egypt, United Arab Emirates, Saudi Arabia), and Asia (Russia, China, Kazakhstan). H&B "corners" are well-defined, smaller sales spaces within department stores and luxury hotels run by prestigious partners all over the world, such as the Palacio de Hierro in Mexico City (Mexico), the Galeries Lafayette in Dubai (United Arab Emirates), Sogo in Hong Kong (China), and The Venetian Hotel in Macao (China).

The latest pillar of the company's marketing strategy consists of building and fostering dialogue and interaction with customers all over the world. Collectively, the products, branding, and stores make up a magical triad, as identified by H&B's CEO, necessary for building and maintaining a "tacit" dialogue with customers. Additionally, personal pages on social networks enable interaction and appraisal of needs and suggestions. The development of these four pillars has enabled Harmont & Blaine Spa to achieve significant growth rates from 2001 to the present (Fig. 2.6). In 2015, revenues amounted to €74.8 million for Harmont & Blaine Spa, € 1.1 million for Harmont & Blaine Switzerland, and €0.3 million for Harmont & Blaine France. The revenues for the Junior and shoes categories were €12 million and €8 million, respectively (Interview with Domenico Menniti, 2016 and Marco Montefusco, 2015).

Table 2.4 provides a detailed view of H&B's key business indices from 2009 to 2014. Specifically, despite the worldwide economic crisis, EBITDA (Earnings before Interest, Taxes, Depreciation, and Amortization) amounted to €7.4 million (9.9 % of revenues) in 2014, compared to €11.8 million (18.4 % of revenues) in 2013. EBIT (Earnings before Interest and Taxes) amounted to €4.5 million (6 % of net sales) (Harmont & Blaine, 2015a).

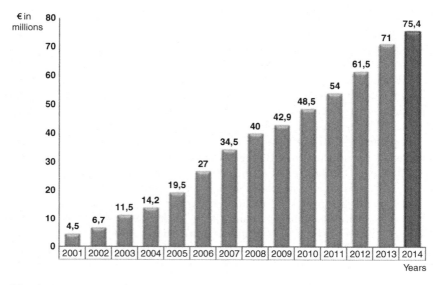

Fig. 2.6   Revenues of Harmont & Blaine Spa from 2001 to 2014 (*Note*: Harmont & Blaine, 2015 annual report)

Table 2.4   Key business indices of Harmont & Blaine from 2009 to 2014

	2009	2010	2011	2012	2013	2014
EBITDA (% on turnover)	17	21	18	16	18.4	10
EBIT (% on turnover)	14	18	11	12	14	6
ROE (%)	21.83	16.95	19.1	12.5	19.7	5.87
ROI (%)	9.52	8.92	10.9	4.23	11.3	5.88

Note: Harmont & Blaine, 2015 annual report

The trend of financial performance shown in Table 2.4 highlights a decrease consistent with the general trend of international fashion and luxury. Nevertheless, the table shows significant growth of ROI in 2013, contrasting the overall industry's decreasing performance.[12] Furthermore, H&B has opened 10 new stores in the past 3 years (Fashion and Luxury Insight Report 2015). H&B's main market in Italy comprised 81 % of revenue (€59.3 million) in 2014, an increase of 3.7 % from 2013 (€57.1 million) (Harmont & Blaine, 2015a). H&B's financial performance and

Table 2.5 Awards given to Harmont & Blaine

Years	Organizations and research institutes	Awards
2012	Cribis, D&B	Company with the highest business reliability
2010	Industrial Union of Naples	Innovative company
2008	Ernst & Young	Businessman of the Year
2008	Pambianco	Company with the highest growth rate
2008	Dun & Bradstreet	Company with the highest reliability
2007	Confindustria (Confederation of Italian Industry)	Excellence of Made in Italy
2006	Eurispes	Italian Excellence
2006	Pambianco/Il Sole 24 Ore	Company with the highest growth rate
2005	Unicredit Bank	Champion of Italian Excellence

Note: Harmont & Blaine, 2015 annual report

international growth have drawn the attention of organizations and research institutions, yielding several awards for the company (Table 2.5).

COMPANY HISTORY

The company began as a family business in 1986 under the name PDM, created by four brothers named Domenico and Enzo Menniti and Paolo and Massimo Montefusco.[13] PDM initially produced leather gloves primarily through OEM, an old family tradition and a quintessential product from the Naples area. However, in the early 1990s, prompted by a series of negative events and changes in consumer lifestyles, PDM decided to extend its product range with high-quality ties and register a new brand called "Harmont & Blaine," its logo identified by a small dachshund. The brand's name and image recalls the legendary Duke of Harmont, who in 1700 used to travel together with his dog Blaine to search for fine fabric that he later brought to Neapolitan tailors to produce elegant and unique clothing. Furthermore, the dachshund is known to be an excellent bloodhound with a keen nose and sharp intelligence.

Nevertheless, fashion trends were hard to predict: avant-garde stylists declared the tie "out of style." The company again declined due to a negative sales trend. The four brothers then decided to focus their core business on the production of clothing for men. A funny and colorful collection of men's swimming trunks served as their first attempt to redirect the company.

Positive market responses encouraged the firm to extend its range of products again. Taking advantage of creative insights from retailers and the entrepreneurial intuition of the founders, the company presented in Capri the first "Harmont & Blaine" shirt collection in 1995, thus entering a new business area and positioning its products strategically between the well-known sport style of Ralph Lauren and the stylish and expensive Façonnable.[14] The "Harmont & Blaine" shirt collection led to a true breakthrough in the fashion world of the 1990s, a time when elegance was identified uniquely by absolute and dark colors, such as grey and black. H&B's shirts were colorful and fashionable, proposing a new multi-chromatic and smart clothing style that invoked the tailored elegance of Made in Italy. Furthermore, the products retained the typical sartorial technique, guaranteeing softness and wearability.

In the following years, the brand's visibility and reputation increased considerably, during which the company expanded both in Italy and abroad by opening its own mono-brand boutiques: the first opened in the province of Naples in April 2000, followed by several others throughout Italy and in Miami in 2001. To build upon its steady brand identity, the firm changed its name from PDM to Harmont & Blaine Spa in 2006. The fit between brand name and company name functioned as a message of transparency and perfect compatibility between the brand and company values, a reinterpretation of traditional *Made in Italy* quality according to innovative and creative designs.

In 2009, the firm launched the "Harmont & Blaine Cafè" project with the creation of coffee shops. This initiative allowed the firm to expand its business not only to sell sandwiches, croissants, and coffee, but more so to offer its consumers pleasant places where they could relax. In effect, the firm pursued its wider aim of enhancing the value proposition for its customers.

Two years later, in response to remarkable opportunities regarding collaboration and partnership, the firm engaged in co-branding activity with Honda Automobili Italia SpA, which led to the creation of the first Honda "CR-V 4WD limited edition by Harmont & Blaine." This collaboration enhanced the brand's visibility, increased brand awareness, and strengthened its brand positioning (Interview with Domenico Menniti, 2015).

In 2014, H&B opened its first online boutique and created several pages on social media (Facebook, Twitter, LinkedIn, YouTube, and Instagram) to dialogue interactively with consumers through the sharing of updated information, experiences, and ideas while also receiving suggestions and fruitful insights.

In February 2014, H&B finally closed the "Chinese battle" regarding illegal uses of its brand name and logo that severely undermined the brand's reputation and revenues in China.[15] The brand has been widely counter-feited in the past few years. As affirmed by CEO Domenico Menniti,

> Since 2008, the company has been involved in over 800 criminal acts following seizures of Harmont & Blaine products. In January 2016, police have also confiscated an unauthorized boutique with the Harmont & Blaine sign and many fake products in Lebanon. For the brand's protection, the company has strengthened collaboration with the police, its monitoring systems, and the quality of its products in order to make them even more recognizable by the customer. (Interview with Domenico Menniti, 2016)

In 10 years of legal disputes, H&B closed its 12 boutiques and halted agreement with its local partners. Only after the Chinese Patent Office recognized the rights of this international brand to the Harmont & Blaine society did H&B relaunch these 12 boutiques and reopen five mono-brand stores selling "Harmont & Blaine Junior." Figure 2.7 summarizes Harmont & Blaine's milestones from 1986 to the present.

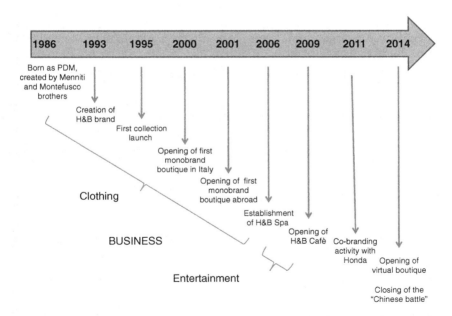

Fig. 2.7 Milestones of Harmont & Blaine (*Note*: Authors based on trade publications and corporate website)

The Harmont & Blaine Branding Strategy

The creation and communication of a strong and internationally recognized brand has been one of the most important strategic objectives pursued by the company's founders since 1993. Strong brand identity (Abratt & Kleyn, 2012; Keller, Busacca, & Ostillio, 2005) and brand equity (Yoo, Donthu, & Lee, 2000) are extremely critical, which explains why H&B has devoted various efforts to such developments since 1993. Strong brand identity emerges as the result of managing four aspects of corporate branding: visual identity, brand promise, brand personality, and brand communication (Abratt & Kleyn, 2012). The following explains how H&B performed in each aspect.

Visual Identity

Visual identity enhances recognition and association abilities of stakeholders, enabling them to associate an experience with a specific brand and to develop a perception of the organization's reputation over time (Abratt & Kleyn, 2012). Visual identity depends on three elements: the brand name, logo, and color (Abratt & Kleyn, 2012; Melewar & Saunders, 1998). The most significant element of H&B's visual identity has proven to be its logo: the dachshund (Fig. 2.8). This symbol quintessentially reflects the company's philosophy and values, since the dachshund is an excellent bloodhound known for developing keen instincts and intelligence that compensate for its small size and short legs. Similarly, the firm might be said to have hone its senses and intelligence to penetrate the Italian fashion market successfully during times of economic crisis. The original color of the brand name and logo was blue (Fig. 2.3), meant to express dependability, trustworthiness, and high quality. However, grey,

Fig. 2.8   Logos and symbol colors by Harmont & Blaine brands (*Note*: Authors based on corporate website)

yellow, and red-purple have since been used to differentiate the main brand name from its more economical product lines: Harmont & Blaine Jeans and Harmont & Blaine Sport. These colors bring associations with dependability, high quality, happiness, and inexpensiveness. Gray and fuchsia distinguish the Harmont & Blaine Café brand.

Brand Promise

The brand promise is both functional and emotional (Abratt & Kleyn, 2012), guaranteeing satisfactory value relevant for customers and other stakeholders (Hameide, 2011). The Harmont & Blaine promise also reflects a set of functional and experiential features (Fig. 2.9).

Functional features are based on the quality/peculiarity of raw materials and processing techniques. The H&B brand evokes fine fabric (e.g., pure silk, cotton, linen, cashmere), special attention to detail (e.g., the dachshund logo on all products is embroidered), and quality stitching and finishing. High levels of quality are guaranteed by outsourcing production only from selected Neapolitan craft businesses. The expertise and know-how of these business partners form a crucial point of trust for the creation of luxury products characterized by high quality and a continuous search for new textile solutions. For example, recent news concerns a reversible and waterproof jacket for women completely realized in pure silk in the fabrics, padding, and buttons.

Emotional benefits concern the lifestyle proposed by the firm and its *Made in Italy* concept: "The firm is not only a leader in the search for new methods of using clothes and colors, but also in the offering of a new style

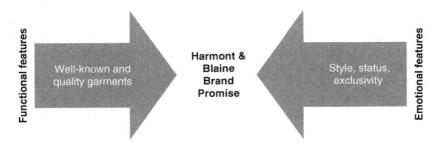

Fig. 2.9 Promise of Harmont & Blaine (*Note*: Developed by authors based on Abratt and Kleyn (2012))

that meets the needs of those people that in clothing look for new elements of design and functionality" (Harmont & Blaine, 2015a). All product lines express a value proposition packed with experiential and emotional attributes that recall a lifestyle with which the customer prefers to identify himself/herself. These features are based on a winning mixture of colors, clothes, and nuances that has revolutionized monochrome casual clothing: "*Models, clothes, buttons, and accessories are combined to create something unique*" (Harmont & Blaine, 2013). H&B has indeed achieved true breakthrough into traditional styles for men, for instance proposing polo-shirts with patterned details (neck and turn up) and shirts with stripes and flowers.

Daring creativity, trendiness, and smart elegance define the essence of the H&B brand promise. It offers not only a fashion product, but also a lifestyle: "*We offer a line of clothing coherent with the lifestyle of people that wish to express their personality in what they wear*" (Harmont & Blaine, 2015a). It promises a combination of ideas, emotions, and experiences: "*elements of coherence respecting the lifestyle they aspire to*" (Harmont & Blaine, 2015a).

Brand Personality

Personality is linked to the brand's emotional characteristics (Mindrut, Manolica, & Roman, 2015), expressing the feelings, thoughts, and actions of the whole firm (Keller & Richey, 2006). It reflects the set of human characteristics associated with a brand (Aaker, 1997). H&B's brand conveys a strong personality reinforced by its products, founders, and the actions taken by the company. It also evokes the characteristics of sincerity, competence, excitement, and sophistication (Fig. 2.10). The first brand characteristic of H&B, its sincerity, is linked both to the honesty and morality of its founders and the cheerfulness of its products. Messages of honesty and morality emerge from the slogan, "From Naples it's possible," a slogan chosen by company founders to highlight the possibility of conducting business with honesty and without compromise, even in a location known for crime. The sincerity of this brand also emerges from its cheerful collections, which exalt the colors of the Mediterranean.

The next characteristic, the competence of the brand, emerges from tradition and collaboration. Its success, indeed, is highly dependent on a strong textile tradition and highly specialized SMEs' that produce for famous brands and foster collaboration among them to serve the entire supply chain. Collaboration also embodies the H&B

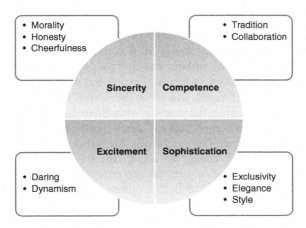

Fig. 2.10 Personality of Harmont & Blaine (*Note*: Developed by the authors based on Aaker (1997))

philosophy. Employees are accustomed to teamwork and harbor a strong group identity: they are part of a "family," as H&B's CEO loves to say. For 5 years, the company has implemented "people satisfaction action," aimed at motivating and giving gratification to the staff on the basis of a reward system. However, the true point of strength depends on a multi-year relationship with employees: to show gratitude to their employees, H&B provides grants to the design academy for deserving children of employees. The purpose of this action is twofold: (i) it strengthens the bond between company and employee, and (ii) it teaches skills to young people with the potential to be employed by the company. Furthermore, the company supports the families of employees during health-related and economic difficulties.

Third, the excitement of the brand emerges from the daring of its founders and their ability to cope with negative events and changes in consumer lifestyles. Over time, they successfully identified new market opportunities, deciding for instance to produce ties and shirts and to offer "total look" products for men. For this reason, H&B has proven to be a dynamic brand able to capture new trends and consumer needs. The company offers more than 10,000 polo models and about 750 shirt models. The CEO loves to tell about the launch of the first collection of shirts in the early 1990s. To cope with the drastic reduction in market consumption of gloves, the company decided to make a breakthrough by launching a collection, completely unconventional, that could capture *innovator customers* who were tired of the black and white colors that predominated fashion collections at that time. However, in the early 1990s, the range of textile fibers was not that rich or varied. The fabrics differed by quality, craftsmanship, and rarity, but the chromatic universe of patterns was rather limited. As with the Duke of Harmont, the four brothers began searching for novelty with their dachshund logo, but no pattern book met their expectations. They persevered and finally reached an agreement with Inglesina, a company produces baby prams that provided imaginative and daring fabrics, totally new to clothing. Its wearability was further improved after an agreement with a textile company.

The last characteristic of H&B, the sophistication of the brand, is strongly linked to its products, which express elegance, exclusivity, and the Italian style. Fine and innovative fabric, attention to detail, and quality of stitching and finishing make H&B products synonymous with Italian excellence.

Brand Communication

Brand communication functions as the key element when managing brand relationships with customers, employees, suppliers, retailers, media, and the community (Zehir, Sahina, Kitapc, & Özsahin, 2011). H&B's communication always aims to link feelings of quality, prestige, and style with the brand. The company thus allocated about 9 % of its revenue to communication activities until it was reduced to 3 % this year due to the global economic crisis (Interview with Domenico Menniti, 2015). Based on Van Riel (1995), H&B's communication activities are categorized as (i) organizational communication with various stakeholders, (ii) management communication within the company, and (iii) marketing communication with consumers to foster product sales.

First, organizational communication with stakeholders stimulates interest, attention, wide consensus, and approval from the media for the brand, products, company, and founders. These activities consist of public relations, sponsorships, corporate advertising, and advertising partnerships with celebrities. In particular, the involvement of about 30 celebrities over time with both formal and informal agreements[16] from the world of fashion, sport, and entertainment has contributed to strengthened brand awareness, brand image and consumer perceptions, as celebrities are typically associated with a "quality guarantee." The H&B brand has been associated with success and good fortune thanks to Italian soccer player Fabio Cannavaro, who became

Fig. 2.11 Harmont & Blaine's fashion night events (*Note*: Harmont & Blaine official Facebook page)

the official testimonial of the company and in 2006 won the title of World Champion, as well as the prestigious recognitions of the Golden Ball and FIFA World Player. Furthermore, each firm's activities, such as the opening of a new store, the promotion of a new collection, or the organization of a fashion event, serves as an influential means of communication to reinforce brand image and diffuse the brand's essence as aligning with the Mediterranean lifestyle. Moreover, "fashion nights" at its exclusive boutiques celebrate the Mediterranean and Italian lifestyle evoked by the brand (Fig. 2.11). Social media complete the communication plan designed by the firm, supporting and integrating the issues communicated by the corporate website. Each type of social media provides interaction with a multitude of stakeholders and allows information to be updated in real time. H&B uses the company website and social network pages as storytelling tools to illustrate the brand's history and values (Russo Spena, Colurcio, & Melia, 2013).

Second, management communication aims to strengthen the organization's group identity and engage all employees in the sharing of values, missions, and objectives. Despite its market performance and its large size, H&B, like many large Italian firms that began as family businesses, maintains a family leadership style, and prioritizes the affection of employees toward the company. The strong link between the company and its employees was demonstrated by huge efforts made by the founders not to dismiss employees during the crisis of the late 1980s. Employees reciprocate the relationship through maximum commitment on special occasions, such participation in events, new openings, and the launch of

Fig. 2.12   Harmont & Blaine articles in leading newspapers (*Note:* Harmont & Blaine website)

new collections. On these occasions, all employees collaborate to maximize results, regardless of rewards: "Cooperation is in the DNA of Harmont & Blaine" (Interview with Domenico Menniti, 2015). The main tool by which to achieve people's satisfaction is dialogue, through formal and informal meetings. Some incentives reward commitment to achieving company and departmental goals.

Third, marketing communication activities are consistent with corporate communication objectives. Advertising mainly stresses well-defined moments of the firm's life, such as the launch of a new collection, the inauguration of a new boutique, the promotion of fashion events, and participation in influential fashion events. Advertising in daily newspapers and magazines worldwide (Fig. 2.12) also supports institutional communication. Product placement is another way to promote the brand. H&B products have appeared in numerous TV and cinema productions. Outdoor advertising is a traditional communication tool used mainly by H&B to spread brand knowledge and enhance brand image. It was used effectively in China when it expanded markets there (Fig. 2.13).

Fig. 2.13 Outdoor advertising of Harmont & Blaine in China (*Note*: Harmont & Blaine website)

Conclusion and Implications

The fashion industry has become highly competitive (Bhardwaj & Fairhurst, 2010) and requires rapid responsiveness (Wheelright & Clark, 1992) to consumers' ever-changing lifestyles. H&B illustrates the evolution of an Italian family business into one that has established a successful brand identity all over the world. H&B offers a creative and casual style that expresses smart elegance; the brand prioritizes fine fabrics such as pure silk, cotton, linen, and cashmere, special attention to detail, and quality stitching and finishing. All marketing actions aim to enhance the brand's reputation and image. Brand name, logo (the dachshund dog), and colors all contribute strongly to brand identity as powerful symbols of the firm's philosophy and values. The brand's functional and emotional promise—along with its evocative personality, expression of dynamism, passion, tradition, and exclusivity—favors the creation and strengthening of brand identity. Also, the opening of exclusive stores and flagship stores in "fashion world centres" has contributed to enhancement of brand identity as well (Abratt & Kleyn, 2012; Moore, Doherty, & Doyle, 2010). Over the years, H&B has created positive associations related to high quality and brand loyalty and therefore enjoys a strong reputation and image in the international fashion scene.

H&B's competitive strength has depended mainly on its marketing strategy of four pillars that increase brand awareness (Aaker, 1997) and sustain superior performance. Its excellence infuses strong *Made in Italy* traits into the products by reinterpreting the sartorial tradition through creative designs. As H&B works essentially through subcontractors, this allows for collaborative relationships, as the production director is strongly engaged in the periodic assessment of subcontractors and in training the workers. At the beginning of every new collection's production, subcontractors are trained on fabrics and techniques for specific markets and/or customer targets. All products are managed according to a checklist set up by H&B production staff. The need for trustworthy relationships (Gummesson, 2004) is also critical considering the confidentiality required for the deployment of new collections, in terms of colors, patterns, typology of items, fabric, and yarns. Collaboration with fabric suppliers is also important for quality excellence: suppliers are often sources of innovation through the proposition of new solution for yarn and fabric and new opportunities that improve the functional quality of products. Such collaboration enables for learning processes, as different actors work together to integrate resources, knowledge, expertise, and creativity to produce value and innovation (Lusch & Numbisan, 2015).

Cooperation with downstream partners is also critical for the development and protection of brand image for companies like H&B that use significant portions of stores that are not managed directly by H&B. H&B fosters long-lasting relationships with retailers and promotes a favorable reward policy with them (Guercini, 2001). Retailers, department stores, and hotels are H&B partners whom the marketing director visits periodically. Their merchandising, in-store communication actions, and promotions are arranged with the company; recently, H&B has developed a *loyalty agenda* to motivate and reward its retailing partners.

The case of H&B offers important lessons for SMEs. First, H&B shows that SMEs can perform high quality production while working with subcontractors and fabric providers who strategically achieves a high standard of quality and prompts innovation (Colurcio, 2009). The collaboration reaches beyond business boundaries and prioritizes the sharing of information, knowledge, and competences with new actors (Caridà, Melia, & Colurcio, 2016). Another lesson to SMEs is the need for strategic planning of international expansion. The problems that H&B experienced with counterfeit goods in the Chinese market highlighted the company's oversight. At the beginning, the four brothers were flattered by number of H&B fakes and underestimated their negative effects. The deployment of timely suitable strategies for brand protection, such as awareness campaigns and focused advertising, could have reduced the decrease in revenue.

H&B has coped with challenges thanks to the entrepreneurial insights of its founders. Its communication, however, is not part of its strategic planning. Incidences of unplanned promotion efforts include giving an annual wardrobe of shirts to well-known figures (actors, soccer players, showmen, etc.) at their peak of fame. Such actions do not guarantee systemic effects and depend on the willingness of the spokesperson. From this, a critical question emerges: is such action sustainable without adopting a strategic long-term plan of communication? An additional consideration relates to the increasing diffusion of digital and smart technologies. Companies are compelled to manage their brands digitally, implying the need for developing platforms, to which H&B might dedicate its resources as well.

NOTES

1. The Neapolitan school was founded in 1351 with the foundation of the Brotherhood of Tailors and reached its peak in the period during which Naples was the capital of the two Sicilies, as well as a socioeconomic and fashion center reference point rivalling London and Paris. In 1611, 607 tailors in Naples were approved to do the work and recognized by The Brotherhood. In 1887, a Neapolitan tailor wrote the treatise "The Art of the cut," receiving international recognition. To date, the Neapolitan tailoring tradition has become renowned all over the world, as demonstrated by a recent article published by the Financial Times (January 27, 2015): "If Italy is a study in contrasts, Naples and its tailors provide one of the most striking. While the southern city is racked by decline and urban decay, some of its streets in the grip of organised crime, the fortunes of its tailors—whose hand-cut, hand sewn suits fit with the city's languor and regal beauty — are rising" (Sanderson, 2015).
2. The D & B rating expresses a synthetic and predictive ranking of reliability on the overall situation of the company, with a 1 to 4 scale (1 = the highest rating of reliability of the company).
3. Since 2005, AGB Company produces for Harmont & Blaine's junior line through an exclusive subcontractor's agreement.
4. In 2016, two new subsidiaries will be established, one in the United States and the other in Spain, responsible for the activities of four boutiques (Madrid, Barcelona, Puerto Banus, and Malaga), 15 corners in El Corte Ingles, and 3/4 outlets (Interview with Domenico Menniti, 2015).
5. In Campania, the three main Italian textile districts are located in:
   1) San Giuseppe Vesuviano (the largest textile district of South Italy, with more than 4,000 companies specializing in the production of clothing for men, women, and children, as well as fabrics, curtains, etc.),
   2) Sant'Agata dei Goti-Casapulla (focused on the production of jackets, slacks, knitwear, shirts, and leather clothing), and
   3) San Marco dei Cavoti (specializing in some phases of production, such as the cutting of fabrics and packaging of the garments).
6. Marinella is a Naples-based third-generation company with over 100 years of history producing tailored, high-quality, and handmade ties that are sold through six exclusive boutiques (located in Naples, Milan, London, Tokyo, Hong Kong, and Lugano) and several corner shops located in Europe, Asia (Isetan-Japan) and America (New York and Washington, United States). Among the most famous customers of the company are all the United States Presidents from Kennedy to Bill Clinton, as well as Re Juan Carlos and Prince Alberto II of Monaco.
7. Kiton produces mainly high-quality, custom-tailored, and handmade dresses, which require 25 to 50 hours of work. All products are sold through

boutiques in Europe (Paris, London, Barcelona, Vienna), Asia (Moscow, Singapore, Tokyo), the United States (Miami, New York, San Francisco, Houston), and the Middle East (Dubai, Abu Dhabi).

8. The Harmont & Blaine café revenue in 2013 amounted to €555,000 (up 121 % compared to €250,703 for 2012) (Harmont & Blaine, 2013). However, at present the firm has decided to concentrate its efforts exclusively on its core business.

9. For the project "Global Cities" by the end of 2016, the company has planned openings in cities like London, New York, Tokyo, and Singapore (Interview with Domenico Menniti, 2015).

10. For example, during the Moscow store inauguration, all the shop windows emphasized the cultural link between Italy and Russia through the representation of three classic dancers in the colors of the Russian flag, a sport in which both countries have always excelled.

11. In this way the company controls the flow of unsold stock, monitors the brand appeal, and increases short-term liquidity (Interview with Domenico Menniti, 2015).

12. The industry's profitability declined. In 2013, the average ROI fell by 1.5 %, compared to the previous year (Fashion and Luxury Insight Report—SDA Bocconi, 2015).

13. The four founders are brothers by their mother, who was married to Sir Montefusco as her second husband.

14. Founded in Nice, France in 1950, Façonnable is an international company that distributes its products in Europe, North and South America, Middle East, Asia, and Africa. Façonnable is a high-end brand renowned worldwide for its timeless collections for men and women.

15. The usurpation of the brand is widespread in China. When Italian companies enter the Chinese market, they often find that some Chinese company has already filed the same brand. China applies the principle of "first to file," for which the trade mark right is given to the subject who submitted the request first. There are cases in which Chinese entrepreneurs have acquired the ownership of Italian trademarks, taking advantage of the reputation or trying to sell them to the Italian owner. These "shadow companies" are mainly located in Hong Kong, where the constitution paperwork and company registration are particularly rapid and where the local trademark office does not perform background searches or checks on lists of filed trademarks. Italian companies generally have no alternative but to pay. Harmont & Blaine instead has chosen the path of litigation, by resorting to the Chinese Department of Appeal of the Patent Office, which upheld the claim and assigned the exclusive right to the brand Harmont & Blaine. The decision is now final (Interview with Domenico Menniti, 2016).

16. Informal agreements concern all moments in which well-known national and international brand lovers contribute to enhance brand image as they participate in important moments of the firm's life, such as the opening of a new store, the promotion of a new collection, the organization of a fashion event, or simply the purchase of Harmont & Blaine products. Among these international celebrities are actors such as Sylvester Stallone, Antony Delon, Kevin Spacey, Helen Hunt, Beyonce, Jay-Z, and Massimiliano Rosolino (swimmer and Italian Olympic champion).

REFERENCES

Aaker, J. L. (1997). Dimensions of brand personality. *Journal of Marketing Research, 34*(3), 347–356. doi:10.2139/ssrn.945432

Abratt, R., & Kleyn, N. (2012). Corporate identity, corporate branding and corporate reputations: Reconciliation and integration. *European Journal of Marketing, 46*(7/8), 1048–1063. doi:10.1108/03090561211230197

Bhardwaj, V., & Fairhurst, A. (2010). Fast fashion: response to changes in the fashion industry. *The International Review of Retail, Distribution and Consumer Research, 20*(1), 165–173. doi:10.1080/09593960903498300

Caridà, A., Melia, M., & Colurcio, M. (2016). Business model design and value co-creation. Looking for a new pattern. In T. R. Spena, C. Mele, & M. Nuutinen (cur.), *Co-innovating: activity, practice, learning and social context in innovation* (pp. 339–364). Cham, Switzerland: Springer.

Colurcio, M. (2009). TQM: a knowledge enabler?. *The TQM Journal, 21*(3), 236–248. doi:10.1108/17542730910953013

Fashion & Luxury Insght. (2015). Report – Altagamma Bocconi. *SDA BOCCONI*. Milan, Italy.

Guercini, S. (2001). Relation between branding and growth of the firm in new quick fashion formulas: analysis of an Italian case. *Journal of Fashion Marketing and Management: An International Journal, 5*(1), 69–79. doi:10.1108/EUM0000000007280

Gummesson, E. (2004). Return on relationships (ROR): the value of relationship marketing and CRM in business-to-business contexts. *Journal of Business & Industrial Marketing, 19*(2), 136–148. doi:10.1108/08858620410524016

Hameide, K. (2011). *Fashion branding unraveled*. New York: Fairchild Books.

Harmont & Blaine. (2013). Bilancio Consolidato al 31 dicembre 2013. Retrieved from http://www.harmontblaine.it/

Harmont & Blaine. (2015a). Company profile October 2015. Retrieved from http://www.harmontblaine.it/

Harmont & Blaine. (2015b). Annual report. Retrieved from http://www.harmontblaine.it/

Hamont & Blaine Facebook. (2015). In *Facebook* [Official company page]. Retrieved from https://www.facebook.com/HarmontBlaine/

Harmont & Blaine Website. (2015). Retrieved from http://www.harmontblaine.it/

Keller, K. L., Busacca, B., & Ostillio, M. C. (2005). *La gestione del brand. Strategie e sviluppo.* Milan, Italy: Egea.

Keller, K. L., & Richey, K. (2006). The importance of corporate brand personality traits to a successful 21st century business. *Journal of Brand Management, 14*(1/2), 74–81. doi:10.1057/palgrave.bm.2550055

Lusch, R. F., & Nambisan, S. (2015). Service innovation: a service-dominant logic perspective. *MIS Quarterly, 39*(1): 155–175.

Melewar, T. C., & Saunders, J. (1998). Global corporate visual identity systems: standardization, control and benefits. *International Marketing Review, 15*(4), 291–308. doi:10.1108/02651339810227560

Melia, M., Colurcio, M., & Caridà, A. (2014). In-store communication to improve the customer experience. *International Journal of Applied Behavioral Economics, 3*(4), 55–70. doi:10.4018/ijabe.2014100104

Mindrut, S., Manolica, A., & Roman, C. T. (2015). Building brands identity. *Procedia Economics and Finance, 20*, 393–403. doi:10.1016/S2212-5671(15)00088-X

Moore, M. C., Doherty, A. M., & Doyle, S. A. (2010). Flagship stores as a market entry method: The perspective of luxury fashion retailing. *European Journal of Marketing, 44*(1/2), 139–161. doi:10.1108/03090561011008646

Russo Spena, T., Colurcio, M., & Melia, M. (2013). Storytelling e web communication. *Mercati e Competitività, 5*, 99–119. doi:10.3280/MC2013-001007

Sanderson, R. (2015). Tailors from Naples are back in style. *Financial Times.* Retrieved from http://www.ft.com/cms/s/0/50879ef0-a314-11e4-9c06-00144feab7de.html#slide0

Van Riel, C. (1995). *Principles of corporate communication.* Hemel Hempstead: Prentice Hall.

Wheelright, S., & Clark., K. (1992). *Revolutionizing product development: quantum leaps in speed, efficiency, and quality.* New York: The Free Press.

Yoo, B., Donthu, N., & Lee, S. (2000). An examination of selected marketing mix elements and brand equity. *Journal of the Academy of Marketing Science, 28*(2), 195–211. doi:10.1177/0092070300282002

Zehir, C., Sahina, A., Kitapç, H., & Özsahin, M. (2011). The effects of brand communication and service quality in building brand loyalty through brand trust; the empirical research on global brands. *Procedia Social and Behavioral Sciences, 24*, 1218–1231. doi:10.1016/j.sbspro.2011.09.142

Dr. Maria Colurcio is associate professor at the University Magna Graecia of Catanzaro, Italy, where she teaches marketing and innovation management. Her current research interests include value co-creation and service innovation. She has published research papers in well-established journals such as Journal of Service Management, Journal of Service Marketing, Managing Service Quality.

Dr. Monia Melia is currently a postdoctoral research fellow at the University Magna Graecia of Catanzaro, Italy, where she received her PhD in Economic and Management of Healthcare in 2011. She also teaches marketing at the university. Her research interests are retail marketing, service innovation and digital marketing. She has authored refereed publications in national and international books and journals.

CHAPTER 3

Salvatore Ferragamo: Brand Heritage as Main Vector of Brand Extension and Internationalization

Maria Carmela Ostillio and Sarah Ghaddar

Abstract As with many other family businesses that collectively comprise Italy's economic fabric, Salvatore Ferragamo began as a workshop that soon grew into a global player within its industry, all while maintaining a core spirit of familial entrepreneurship in the form of its organizational structure and identity. Today, the company operates in over 90 countries via its own 33 subsidiaries. The Salvatore Ferragamo Group has pursued a coherent corporate branding strategy over time. Its brand heritage serves as an intrinsic feature of its value proposition and brand positioning, having been cohesively maintained even amid brand extensions and internationalization. Leveraging this heritage, the company has evolved during its 88-year-long history from a

M.C. Ostillio (✉)
SDA Bocconi School of Management, Milan, Italy

S. Ghaddar
Department of Marketing – Claudio Dematté Research, SDA Bocconi
School of Management, Milan, Italy

© The Author(s) 2017
B. Jin, E. Cedrola (eds.), *Fashion Branding and Communication*,
Palgrave Studies in Practice: Global Fashion Brand Management,
DOI 10.1057/978-1-137-52343-3_3

single-product company to a multi-category company; from a product-oriented brand to a retail-oriented brand; and from a family business to a publicly owned global business.

Keywords Brand heritage · Brand identity · Brand extension · Internationalization · Corporate branding · Family business

INTRODUCTION

Established in 1928, Salvatore Ferragamo maintains the name of its founder, who was an open-minded shoemaker born in southern Italy. With a sales turnover of €736.1 million in 2014—80 % of which stemmed from exports—the firm currently operates in over 90 countries worldwide, with the Asia-Pacific region constituting its largest share.

The firm's success can be attributed to its brand heritage's function as the main vector of development in both new product launches and new market entry. Brand consistency has been maintained thanks to the business' centralized decision-making approach, within which the Ferragamo family plays the lead role, as well as strong integration between the parent company Salvatore Ferragamo S.p.A. and its broad network of suppliers.

This chapter highlights the Salvatore Ferragamo Group's corporate brand strategy and evaluates three important transitions that the group has made: from a single-product company to a multi-category company, from a product-oriented brand to a retail–oriented brand, and from a family owned business to a publicly traded one. Before introducing the corporate brand strategy, brand positioning, and the key role that brand heritage has played in the strategic process, an overview will be provided about the company history. Some implications useful for researchers and managers, along with future challenges facing the company, will then be provided based on such analyses.

The present case was written based on several interviews with the group's top executives, site visits to the headquarters and the Company Museum, and consultations of various materials, including annual reports, trade and academic journals, books, articles, websites, and mass media sources written in both English and Italian.

COMPANY OVERVIEW

The Italian luxury brand known as the Salvatore Ferragamo Group operates only one brand. Through this corporate brand strategy, the group offers a wide range of product categories for men and women, ranging from footwear, leather goods, apparel, and silk products to jewels, fragrances, and other miscellaneous accessories. This product range also includes eyewear and watches that are manufactured under license by third parties.

The Salvatore Ferragamo Group consists of Salvatore Ferragamo S. p.A. (the Parent company), Ferragamo Parfumes S.p.A. (a subsidiary licensee of the Ferragamo and Ungaro brands for the production and distribution of fragrance products), and 33 subsidiaries that the parent company controls by holding majority stakes, whether directly or indirectly. Salvatore Ferragamo S.p.A., the parent company, is the only manufacturing company in the group, responsible for undertaking production activities and managing the distribution network. Overall, the group employs 3,900 members, including 668 top managers, middle managers and store managers; 2,987 office workers; and 245 workmen/workwomen. The parent company has a total of 880 employees.

Part of the production process is outsourced to external Italian workshops, but the management and organization of the most important stages in the value chain are performed in-house. The group directly manages the first production phases (product development and prototyping), in addition to conducting quality controls during production and on finished products. The strong integration between the Parent company Salvatore Ferragamo S.p.A. and its network of suppliers has enabled broad control to be maintained over the crucial stages of the value chain in the production process. The group possesses an extended distribution network spanning over 90 countries through a direct retail channel, a network of 373 directly operated Ferragamo stores, a wholesale channel comprising a network of 270 mono-brand stores and stores-in-stores managed by third parties, and multi-brand retail channels. The wholesale channel includes department stores, luxury specialist retailers, travel retail/duty free stores inside airports, and franchises that ensure its presence on markets that are not large or developed enough.

The company's total revenue amounts to €1,331.8 million as of 2014, with a growth of 5.9 % compared to 2013. The total revenue from sales corresponds to €736.1 million in 2014, due to an increase of 5.0 % from 2013 (Table 3.1). In terms of total revenue from sales, the Asia Pacific region (30.5 %), together with Japan (6.2 %), accounts for the largest share, followed by Europe (Italy included) (36 %), North America (22. 4 %), and Central and South America (4.6 %) (Table 3.2). The Asia Pacific and Japan also jointly cover 50 % of the firm's overall worldwide network as of December 31, 2014, with Japan representing the highest number of mono brand stores and broadly surpassing the number of stores in Italy. Based on the product portfolio, footwear and leather goods comprised 45 % and 39.3 %, respectively, of the total turnover (Table 3.3). The group currently operates both offline and online, but e-commerce and omni-channel integration actually constitute ongoing challenges for the firm. The e-commerce sites, managed directly by the group, are currently available in several European countries, United States, South Korea, Japan, and Mexico.

COMPANY HISTORY

The 'shoemaker to the stars' Era

Salvatore Ferragamo was born in 1898 in Bonito, a small village in the Southern Italian province of Avellino. As the eleventh of fourteen sons, he served an apprenticeship to a shoemaker in Naples at the age of 11 and quickly opened his own shop in Bonito at the age of 13. Raised in a modest family of farmers, the young Ferragamo, instead of playing with other children his age, would often observe the work of Luigi Festa, the local shoemaker of his hometown. Shoes, along with materials and shapes, already served as his true and natural passion, a passion that even perplexed his parents. To distract their son from his premature obsession, the parents decided to send Salvatore to several apprenticeships—to the barber, to the carpenter and even to the tailor—and yet, Salvatore remained inflexible, fully expressing his unwavering passion with a tenacity that led to his future successes. One day prior to his sister's first communion, when he was 9 years old, Salvatore procured materials from the town's trusted shoemaker and manufactured his first pair of shoes for his sister, since his family's poverty prevented them from buying a traditional pair of white shoes for her ceremony. Seeking to integrate his craftsmanship skills with

Table 3.1 Financial statement of Salvatore Ferragamo, 2010–2014

	2014	2013	2012	2011	2010
Total sales revenues (€million)	736.1	701.2	598.5	526.1	386.6
EBITDA (€million)	168.4 (22.9 % of sales revenues)	153.3 (21.9 % of sales revenues)	104.4 (17.4 % of sales revenues)	81.4 (15.5 % of sales revenues)	54.5 (14.1 % of sales revenues)
Net profits (€million)	107.2	105.5	106.9	76.3	28.4
Export share	81.3 %	82.8 %	82.0 %	84.1 %	84.1 %
Number of employees in the group	3.900	3.764	3.322	3.125	2.827
Number of total stores	643	624	606	593	578
Number of directly operated stores among total stores	373	360	338	323	–
Number of third party operated stores among total stores	270	264	268	270	–

EBITDA: Earnings Before Interest, Taxes, Depreciation and Amortization. *Note*: Developed by the authors based on Salvatore Ferragamo Group annual report 2010–2014

Table 3.2 Sales revenues of Salvatore Ferragamo by geographic area, 2010–2014 (€million)

	2014	2013	2012	2011	2010
Total sales revenues	736.1 (100.0 %)	701.2 (100.0 %)	598.5 (100.0 %)	526.1 (100.0 %)	386.6 (100.0 %)
Italy	138.0 (18.7 %)	120.4 (17.2 %)	107.5 (18.0 %)	83.5 (15.9 %)	61.3 (15.9 %)
Europe	129.5 (17.6 %)	122.0 (17.4 %)	98.1 (16.4 %)	87.8 (16.7 %)	67.5 (17.5 %)
North America	164.6 (22.4 %)	153.4 (21.9 %)	127.0 (21.2 %)	109.6 (20.8 %)	79.3 (20.5 %)
Asia Pacific	224.5 (30.5 %)	215.7 (30.7 %)	191.7 (32.0 %)	175.6 (33.4 %)	121.5 (31.4 %)
Japan	45.3 (6.2 %)	53.3 (7.6 %)	46.5 (7.8 %)	43.6 (8.3 %)	38.7 (10.0 %)
Central and South America	34.2 (4.6 %)	36.4 (5.2 %)	27.7 (4.6 %)	26.0 (4.9 %)	18.3 (4.7 %)

Note: Developed by the authors based on Salvatore Ferragamo Group annual report 2010–2014

Table 3.3 Sales revenues of Salvatore Ferragamo by Products 2010–2014 (€million)

	2014	2013	2012	2011	2010
Total sales revenues	736.1 (100 %)	701.2 (100 %)	598.5 (100 %)	526.1 (100 %)	386.6 (100 %)
Footwear	331.2 (45.0 %)	321.6 (45.9 %)	269.2 (45.0 %)	228.2 (43.4 %)	164.9 (42.7 %)
Leather goods	288.9 (39.3 %)	255.2 (36.4 %)	213.1 (35.6 %)	188.8 (35.9 %)	132.7 (34.3 %)
Apparel	65.8 (8.9 %)	69.7 (9.9 %)	65.3 (10.9 %)	63.2 (12.0 %)	51.6 (13.3 %)
Accessories	50.2 (6.8 %)	54.7 (7.8 %)	50.9 (8.5 %)	45.9 (8.7 %)	37.4 (9.7 %)

Note: Developed by the authors based on Salvatore Ferragamo Group annual report 2010–2014

the new technologies shaping the industry, Salvatore Ferragamo moved to the United States in 1914 at the age of 16, just as World War I broke out in Europe.

At the beginning of the previous century, the United States had been the epicenter of the footwear sector, not only in terms of style, but also in terms of organizational production capacity and structure, as well as manufacturing technology. Major technological change in the leather sector began in the United States during the late eighteenth and early nineteenth centuries, reaching such large-scale development as to guarantee low price production along with high quality tanned leathers. Whereas some European countries, Germany and France in particular, boasted a production capacity comparable to that of the United States, technological change had not yet taken off in Italy. Specifically, central and southern Italy, despite their long tradition in leather processing, still primarily used the slow tanning in pits system, a method soon to be replaced worldwide by the tanning drum—a new system allowing for a drastic reduction of production time from 8 months to 48 hours. This technological gap resulted in slow production time and low profits for the Italian industry.

For Salvatore Ferragamo, moving to the United States meant a broadening of horizons, beyond the limits of his homeland; it meant experiencing ideas without cost limitations. Once in the United States, he met with one of his brothers who worked in a Boston factory producing shoes branded "Queen Quality." Salvatore worked in this same factory for a brief period after his arrival, after which he quickly moved to Santa Barbara, California, where another brother was living and where his career would soon take off. There, Salvatore Ferragamo opened a shoe repair shop and started working for the America Film Co. and the newly emerging motion picture industry, manufacturing cowboy boots for Western movies and Roman/Greek sandals for the historical films. Working closely with movie directors and actors allowed Salvatore to gain widespread appreciation for the high craftsmanship quality of his shoes. Meanwhile, Salvatore—who was always looking for new means of improvement—studied anatomy at the University of Southern California and focused on the arches of the foot, in order to optimize the fit and comfort of his shoes.

In the early 1920s, the film industry moved to Hollywood, with Salvatore following close behind. The opening of the 'Hollywood Boot Shop' in 1923 marked the launching of Salvatore's "shoemaker to the stars" career, as the local press would come to define him. As various movie "stars" became his regular clients—such as Mary Pickford, Rodolfo

Valentino, John Barrymore Jr., Douglas Fairbanks, and Gloria Swanson, among others—Salvatore's popularity drastically increased. Such fame and press attention helped Salvatore become an accredited fashion maker and provided him with a "voice" in the fashion industry. He gradually modified the rules of fashion concerning women's shoes, altering the style of such footwear and introducing, for instance, the sandals.

In the late 1920s, feelings of homesickness, along with his passion for traditional Italian craftsmanship, put Salvatore Ferragamo back on the way home. The United States had given him access to the newest technology of the period, but it had also deprived him of the traditional craftsmanship to which he was accustomed, due to a scarcity of skilled labor. Once in Italy, Salvatore Ferragamo chose to establish himself in Florence, a town with a long tradition of craftsmanship, and his business soon became increasingly attractive to the international fashion business.

In Florence, Ferragamo found the perfect breeding ground on which to spread his ideas, imbued by a love for materials, details, decorations, embroidery, and lace. Fig. 3.1 shows an example of footwear upper in crochet, realized with a traditional process.

Whereas Ferragamo had been able to implement his ideas without cost concerns in the United States, he was able to bring his imagination to life without limitation in terms of embroideries and precious details in Italy. The strength and added value that characterized the creations of Salvatore Ferragamo combined the most innovative leather produced in foreign

Fig. 3.1   Footwear upper in crochet developed by traditional process (*Source*: Salvatore Ferragamo Museum archive)

tanneries with traditional Italian artisanal techniques, such as embroidery and lace. Meanwhile, his products were exported to the U.S. market to access broader demand. In his new laboratory, he incorporated assembly line production to the traditional artisan manufacturing process, a system that allowed him to cope with the increasing flow of exports to the United States. He also introduced the American system of sizes, in order to manufacture a wide range of foot lengths and widths.

Export flows and business relations with the United States, however, suffered a huge decline during the financial crisis following the Wall Street Crash of 1929, leading him to failure in 1933. The 1930s served as a challenge for Salvatore to reignite his business by acquiring a place in the European market and strengthening its position in the domestic market.

In 1936, Salvatore Ferragamo rented two laboratories along with a shop located inside a historical palace in the center of Florence (Spini Feroni Palace). Overcoming the raw material shortage during World War II with a creative approach, raffia, cellophane, cloth, wire, wood, and synthetic resins became necessary to manufacture the upper of most shoes during the 1940s. At the same time, the heel underwent changes in shape and texture, giving rise to the ever-popular Ferragamo wedge, made with Sardinian cork rather than leather and steel. Increases in success allowed Salvatore in 1938 to pay the first installment for the purchase of the entire Spini Feroni Palace, after which he built a workshop on the first floor and a store on the ground floor. The palace today still hosts the company's headquarters. During the same year, he opened two new branches, one in London and the other in Rome.

In the post-war period, Salvatore Ferragamo's shoes became symbols of Italian style worldwide. These years brought crucial inventions that remain iconic and popular today, such as the metal-reinforced stiletto heels made popular by Marilyn Monroe, as well as gold sandals and invisible sandals with uppers made from nylon fishing line. The latter brought him recognition in the form of the prestigious 'Neiman Marcus Award' in 1947, widely known as the "Academy Award of the fashion world," having been established by Neiman Marcus, one of most popular department stores in the United States. It was the first time that the Award was given to a footwear designer, as well as the first time an Italian was the recipient. The following decades would be the most successful of his career, with Ferragamo gaining the success of a global brand and Spini Feroni Palace representing a popular destination in the international fashion scene.

The film industry and movie stars had not forgotten Ferragamo—celebrities such as Greta Garbo, Sofia Loren, Anna Magnani, the Duke of Windsor, and Audrey Hepburn regularly visited Florence specifically to get their custom craft shoes made in his shop. By 1950, the firm employed 750 people, producing an average of 350 pairs of handmade shoes per day.

Eventually, the processes of industrialization and the transformation of the Italian economy, along with changes to the competitive scenario and the market entry of new footwear manufacturers, collectively encouraged Salvatore Ferragamo to reconsider his production approach. The economic boom began increasing purchasing power, thereby broadening access to the fashion industry. Many firms shifted their market focus from a strictly selective clientele to cater to the rising middle class. During the late 1950s, Salvatore Ferragamo's approach centered on a double line offer—one line focusing on mid-level production with the introduction of a partial mechanical production system, as well as an artisanal line that continued his traditional shoemaker activity. Thus, while continuing to manufacture some handmade shoes, Ferragamo launched two secondary lines, *Ferrina shoes* and *Ferragamo Debs,* which were made in England using a partially mechanical production system (60 % by hand and 40 % by machine).

Furthermore, during the same period, Salvatore Ferragamo began to diversify his product offerings, creating his first bags and printing silk scarves with appealing symbols related to "Italianness." In 1959, he developed a sportswear collection designed by his second daughter Giovanna, who subsequently developed the women's ready-to-wear collection for Lord and Taylor, the oldest luxury department store in North America.

During the 1950s, the company evolved from craftsmanship manufacturing to large-scale production, from a workshop to a company. This period saw the establishment of Ferragamo's brand logo, replacing the original label of "Ferragamo's Creations" with a graphic rendering of the founder's signature. The original dream was fulfilled, but his family would soon pursue a new goal expressed by Salvatore Ferragamo himself: transforming the firm into a total look brand.

The Ferragamo Family Inheritance: Tangible and Intangible Resources

By the time Salvatore Ferragamo died in 1960 at the age of 62, his personal story, along with his own fulfilled dream, was already profoundly linked to the history of Italian fashion. His wife, Miss Wanda, suddenly found herself at the helm of the company, although at the time her "job" entailed being the mother of six children, aged from 3 to 19 years.

The eldest daughter Fiamma (1941–1998)—the only one of Salvatore's six children to have worked closely with their father—became the head of the footwear sector, pioneering a new decision to start industrial production in order to expand distribution and stand up to price competition. Still, she decided also to retain a few manual stages of the manufacturing process. If daily production corresponded to 350 handmade pairs of shoes during the 50's, a decade later it rose to 2000 pairs and became outsourced to small factories in Campania, the Neapolitan region, and Tuscany, the best regions for leather and shoe production. The organizational structure began taking its current shape, being characterized by outsourced production and centralization of the decision-making processes.

In addition, the family confronted the market's lack of confidence in the company's brand potential after Salvatore's death. Continuity in the shoe sector had been possible thanks to a broad archive designed by Salvatore but not yet produced. Initially on her own and later with the support of her sons and daughters, Wanda Ferragamo successfully overcame the difficulties arising from her challenging inheritance, consolidating the company's brand position and reputation while rooting it to its tradition and heritage. Under her direction, the firm made an important transition from a mono-product brand to a multi-category brand. As a result, the company grew into a global commercial distribution, comprising a worldwide network of mono-brand stores and important partnerships with the most qualified multi-brand clients of the fashion retail sector.

Even after production shifted to an industrialized approach and product lines became extended and diversified beyond footwear, the firm preserved certain artisanal aspects of its manufacturing while focusing on details, which still represented key features of the brand's identity. Thus, Ferragamo's family was able to accomplish two key steps of the firm's history—brand extension and global retailing—without betraying the brand's heritage. It retained a respect for the past while also laying the foundation for the future.

From a Family Business Company to a Publicly Traded Company

The late 1990s were years of strong growth and international expansion, signaling the progressive entrance of new management to support the company's growth process. This phase culminated in 2006 with the appointment of a new CEO, Mr. Michele Norsa,[1] who previously had served in top management roles at Benetton, Marzotto, and the Valentino

Fashion Group. Meanwhile, Ferruccio Ferragamo—Salvatore's oldest male son—and Wanda Ferragamo assumed the positions of President and Honorary Chairman of the Group, respectively.

On June 29, 2011, Salvatore Ferragamo S.p.A. went public on the Milan Stock Exchange, finally becoming a publicly traded company. Within the new organizational structure, many of Salvatore Ferragamo's descendants serve as members of the Board of Directors, acting as brand guardians and guarantors of the brand's values.

The Development of the Corporate Brand Strategy

The Ferragamo group reinvented itself by maintaining consistency in its identity and values while also pursing three key transitions: (i) from a single-product to a multi-category company, (ii) from a product-oriented brand to a retail-oriented brand, and (iii) from a family business company to a public company.

One particular aspect of the Salvatore Ferragamo Group is its pursuit of a coherent corporate branding strategy over time, in which it leverages brand heritage as the main vector during brand extension and internationalization. In the next section, the concept of brand heritage is introduced and discussed in the context of Salvatore Ferragamo, while highlighting two key steps of its historical evolution: brand extension and internationalization.

Brand Heritage as a Pillar of the Salvatore Ferragamo Strategy

Any brand (...) can benefit from returning to its roots and identifying what made it special and successful in the first place. A corporate brand usually has roots that are richer and more relevant than those of product brands (Aaker, 2004). Brand heritage refers to

> a dimension of a brand's identity found in its track record, longevity, core values, use of symbols, and particularly in an organizational belief that its history is important. Brand heritage is one way to strengthen corporate-level marketing for those organizations where heritage applies. Heritage is an integrated component of the character of such brands. (Urde, Greyser, & Balmer, 2007, pp. 4–5)

In the customers' point of view, brand heritage can be defined as consumers' perceptions about a brand, as reflected by the brand associations held in consumer memory (Keller, 1993). These associations could be identified as practical needs (e.g., quality, functionality etc.) or as symbolic elements (Bhat & Reddy, 1998; Del Río, Vazquez, & Iglesias, 2001). From a strategic perspective, when a company's brand retains an important historical heritage, this can provide leverage especially in global markets. The next section discusses how the heritage of Salvatore Ferragamo has been uncovered and preserved.

The Brand Heritage: Functional and Symbolic Assets

> There is no limit to beauty, no saturation point in design, no end to the materials a shoemaker may use to decorate his creations so that every woman may be shod like a princess and a princess may be shod like a fairy queen. There is no limit to the materials I have used in these 50 years of shoe-making. I have used diamonds and pearls, real and imitation; gold and silver dust; fine leathers from Germany, Britain, America, and wherever else they may be found. I have used satins and silks, lace and needlework, glass and glass mirrors, feathers. I have used fish, felt, and transparent paper, snail shells and raffia, synthetic silk woven instead of raffia, raw silk, seaweeds and wool. I have used beads, sequins, nylon (which is stronger than leather, notwithstanding its apparent fragility) and sting covered in transparent paper. (Salvatore Ferragamo in his 1957 autobiography, "Shoemaker of Dreams: the Autobiography of Salvatore Ferragamo")

Salvatore's imagination and passion for humble materials and meticulous attention to detail are prominently expressed in two features characterizing his creations: the heel and the upper, which differentiate the brand even today, along with his peculiar use of colors. Salvatore was fascinated by the world of art, specifically by the contemporary movement of historical period in which motions and colors played a central role. This love and curiosity for art led him to build and maintain relationships with several artists involved with the Italian art movement known as Second Futurism. Among them was Giuseppe Landsmann (name art Lucio Venna), who provided four sketches and a manifesto for Salvatore Ferragamo (Fig. 3.2). Venna also created an internal label for the shoes that contained the notice "Ferragamo's Creations Florence Italy," which is still used by the firm today.

The footwear upper constitutes Ferragamo's personal palette and the heel his artistic inclinations. He constantly played with colors and geometric patterns—combining, contouring, and cleaving materials in an endless game of motion, patterns, and shapes. For instance, since the

Fig. 3.2 Venna Manifesto for Salvatore Ferragamo (*Source*: Salvatore Ferragamo Museum archive)

late 1920s, patchwork became one of the *leitmotivs* of his shoe collections, through which he combined leathers and textiles using both tone on tone patterns and different colors. The heel can assume different shapes—a cage, an "F," a wedge, a stiletto, etc.—while being covered with a wide range of different materials (Fig. 3.3). The caged heel, patented in 1955, is equipped with a different textile cover heel to coordinate with dresses according to the specific occasion.

Salvatore Ferragamo reinterprets the humble persona of the traditional shoemaker with intuition, imagination, and creativity. He would often assert that he was not creating "trends," but his style nevertheless continues to influence today's fashion industry. The chromatic composition of his shoes was also quite distinctive, since shoes at the time tended to display mostly muted and neutral colors.

His curiosity further permeated into considerations of shoe functionality and human anatomy. Rather than relying on functional solutions defined by others, he became the first artisan in the footwear sector to

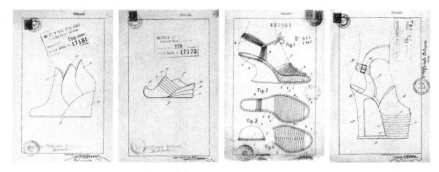

Fig. 3.3   The heel assumes different shapes (*Source*: Salvatore Ferragamo Museum archive)

study the distribution of body weight over the joints of the foot, in order to stabilize the balance of the body and accommodate for natural movement. Over the years, he patented several structural innovations.

Beyond these practical/functional assets, Salvatore Ferragamo had the ability to create the ideal match between a practical/functional asset and its symbolism by placing stress on utopian/mythical assets. Symbolism seemed to be the focus of his communicative approach well before the spread of modern marketing and communication practices. His recurrent use of Feroni Palace in various communicative declinations was not a coincidence. Pietro Annigoni—an Italian portrait and fresco painter—composed a portrait of Spini Feroni Palace during the 1950s to be used on packaging, advertising, and the Ferragamo letterhead. It was also used for one of Ferragamo's first scarves, created in 1961 and still in sale today (Fig. 3.4). The same historical stylized portrait of the Palace was subsequently used in 2011 for the Museo Salvatore Ferragamo exhibition entitled, "Inspiration and Vision."

The launch of the first Ferragamo perfume, supported by strong advertising coverage, was intended to stress this mythic and aesthetic dimension. For instance, the incorporation of mythological characters such as Vulcan[2] and Venus reinforced this mythical dimension as an element characterizing the brand's aesthetic and identity. For this purpose, many photographs portray Salvatore kneeling at the feet of screen "stars" and ordinary women while helping them test the fit of his shoes, as depicted in Fig. 3.5. Table 3.4 features Ferragamo's brand value proposition based on the semiotic analysis of Floch (1990) (Table 3.4).

Fig. 3.4 Salvatore Ferragamo scarf with the print of Spini-Feroni palace (*Source*: Salvatore Ferragamo website (2015). http://www.ferragamo.com. Retrieved December 16, 2015)

The Corporate Museum: Experiencing the Brand's Inheritance
The myth of the brand and customers' awareness of the firm's history and identity are reinforced and perpetuated by the Corporate Museum, within which the concept of brand heritage, in itself an intangible resource, becomes tangible. Corporate museums often focus on tracing the history of the company, highlighting the contributions of the founder and other key individuals, and displaying documents, photographs, and products of

Fig. 3.5   Salvatore Ferragamo at Ladies' feet (*Source*: Salvatore Ferragamo Museum archive)

the past. These museums serve strategic roles in the development of the firm's brand identity and image (Nissley & Casey, 2002).[3]

The Salvatore Ferragamo Museum, opened in May 1995, was created to commemorate the founder's story and the role he played in the history of contemporary footwear and the fashion industry, an aim that aptly reinforces brand identity. Connected to the museum is a center focused

Table 3.4 Salvatore Ferragamo brand value proposition

brand value proposition	
functional dimension	*utopian / mythical dimension*
Salvatore: the artisan, the manufacturer, the shoemaker.	Salvatore: the artist, the shoemaker to the stars, the fulfilled dream.
Functional aspects of footwear and construction techniques (comfort and durability, plumb line, anatomical study, etc.).	Artistic aspects: innovative use of colors and innovative use of materials (fish scales, plexiglass, nylon, gold, etc.).
Practical needs (e.g., quality, functionality). Economic value (e.g., good quality/price ratio).	Symbolic elements: From Bonito (near Naples) to the Palazzo Feroni via Hollywood. Vulcan (Salvatore) and Venus (the screen stars). Symbols related to "Italianness." (e.g., the use of Palazzo Feroni in various communicative declinations).

Note: Developed by the authors based on the semiotic square of consumption values developed by Floch (1990) applied to Salvatore Ferragamo

on the study of footwear, with a library and document archives that reflect the significance attributed to the purely functional aspect of footwear. The collection features 10,000 shoes (including footwear and models), documents, photographs, and shoemaker hacks that document the entire span of Salvatore Ferragamo's career (1927–1960). Some items reveal Salvatore Ferragamo's relationships with art and artists of his day, such as the futurist painter. Others document his continuous quest for the perfect fit and the invention of special constructions and materials, from the famous cork wedge patented in 1936 to the raffia, cellophane vamps, and candy-wrapper paper used during World War II.

In the year 2000, thanks to an important operation involving collaboration among the Ministry for Cultural Assets and Activities, the Ministry for Industry, Trade, and Crafts, and several private organizations, 368 patents and company trademarks registered under the name of Salvatore Ferragamo during 1929–1964 came to light. In the footwear industry, this was the largest number of patents belonging to a single trademark. The Museum is currently researching his activity prior to 1927, when Salvatore worked in the United States as "the stars' shoemaker."

In 1985, in collaboration with the Costume Gallery of the Pitti Palace and the patronage of the Municipality of Florence, the Ferragamo family decided to organize the first retrospective exhibition to commemorate the twenty-fifth anniversary of the founder's death. The exhibition was one of the first in Italy to consider fashion as a phenomenon of culture and contemporary art. The value, quantity, and uniqueness of the available documentation contributed to the eventual decision to convert the exhibition into a permanent museum.

In 1999, in recognition of the museum's cultural worth and its endeavors over the years, the Salvatore Ferragamo Museum received the "Premio Guggenheim Impresa e Cultura," an award given annually to companies that have made the most effective investments in culture. The building was restored in 2000 and now proudly showcases its masterpieces of seventeenth and eighteenth century Florentine art, including frescoes by Bernardino Poccetti in the chapel. Expanded in 2006, the museum actually occupies the basement of the building and comprises seven rooms: the first two being dedicated to the history and work of Salvatore Ferragamo with a 2-year rotating display of his footwear models and the other five hosting 6-month exhibitions organized by the museum on different and unpublished topics. Its goal is to reinterpret, in a modern key, the bond between art, design, costume, and the firm, in addition to fostering connections with leading cultural institutions worldwide. Recent exhibitions have enhanced the link between Salvatore Ferragamo and the world of cinema, as well as the identity and values of the brand. Table 3.5 depicts the main exhibitions hosted in the period of 2010–2015.

Alongside the permanent collection, traveling exhibitions bring the work of Salvatore Ferragamo abroad, raising brand awareness, and promoting its distinctive values all over the world. Among the most famous and successful was a 1998 show at the Sogetsu Foundation Kai in Japan called "A centennial exhibition: Salvatore Ferragamo. The art of the shoe 1927—1960." Another famous one was "Audrey Hepburn. A woman, the style." This exhibition travelled the world between 1999 and 2001, started from the Ferragamo Museum in Florence, and then to the Powerhouse Museum in Sydney, the Nihombashi-Mitsukoshi Museum in Tokyo and Deutsche Filmmuseum in Frankfurt. This attention to a broad audience also takes form in the availability of guides in different languages and the hosting of regular activities and collaborations with local institutions, hotels, tour operators, schools and universities, blogs, bookshops, conferences, seminars, workshops, and archives.

Table 3.5 Exhibitions at Salvatore Ferragamo Museum, 2010–2015

Exhibition	Period	Visitors	Average visitors per month
Greta Garbo	May 13, 2010–October 18, 2010	12,472	2,495
A Regola d'arte	November 18, 2010–May 5, 2011	9,348	1,700
Inspiration and Vision	May 27, 2011–March 12, 2012	24,391	2,567
Secret Archives	March 21, 2012–June 1, 2012	6,590	2,865
Marilyn	June 20, 2012–March 30, 2013	49,178	5,177
The Amazing Shoemaker	April 19, 2013–May 15, 2014	46,651	3,589
Equilibrium	June 19, 2014–April 23, 2015	35,815	3,582

Note: Developed by the authors based on data owned by Salvatore Ferragamo Museum

Brand Heritage as Main Vector of Brand Extension and Internationalization

Salvatore Ferragamo's brand heritage is well reflected by its gradual brand extension process (Fig. 3.6). At first, the firm addressed its products to women, introducing its apparel category along with leather goods (handbags, luggage, belts, wallets and other small leather accessories) in the mid-1960s, followed shortly by the introduction of silk goods and accessories during the early 1970s. The mid-1970s saw the opening of the firm's product offering to a more male audience. From the late 1990s to the present, the firm has progressively introduced complementary categories, such as perfumes and glasses, along with the recent introduction of watches and jewelry. In all of these brand extensions, the group leveraged its established brand image and targeted the same market position as that of the original Salvatore Ferragamo shoes. Ferragamo's original brand concept, described as a balance between eccentricity and elegance, has met the demand of various markets across different dress cultures (Ricci, Morozzi, Ferragamo, & Kung, 2009). From the mid-1980s onward, the Asia Pacific brought the first internationalization efforts undertaken by the firm: Hong Kong in 1986, followed by Japan in 1991, China in 1994, and finally South Korea in 1995. The late 1990s and early 2000s saw entry into Latin America and South Asia, with Mexico City leading the way in 1999, followed by India in 2006. More recent efforts have been directed at Middle Eastern countries, such as United Arab Emirates and Qatar (Fig. 3.7). The group's international markets are primarily operated by 33

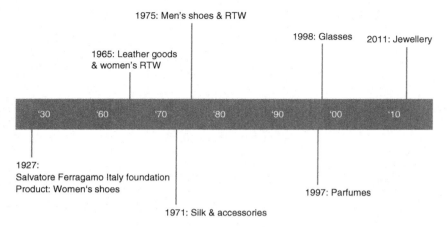

Fig. 3.6 Ferragamo Group's brand extension by time (*Source*: Elaborated by the authors with data published on Salvatore Ferragamo sustainability report 2014)

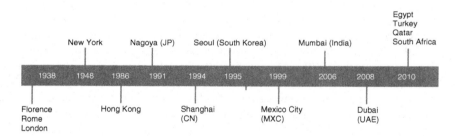

Fig. 3.7 Opening of Directly Operated Stores by time (*Source*: Elaborated by the authors with data published on a PowerPoint presentation by Sofia Ciucchi, Vice President Salvatore Ferragamo)

local subsidiaries located in the main geographic markets: 14 in the Far East, 9 in Europe, and 10 in America (two of which are in liquidation, according to the group's Annual Report on December 31, 2014) (Fig. 3.8).

The Ferragamo group's brand heritage continues in their pursuit of internationalization while adhering to strict standardization in store format and product offerings. Stores are selected on the basis of their coherence with brand positioning in terms of location and visibility. This

Group Structure

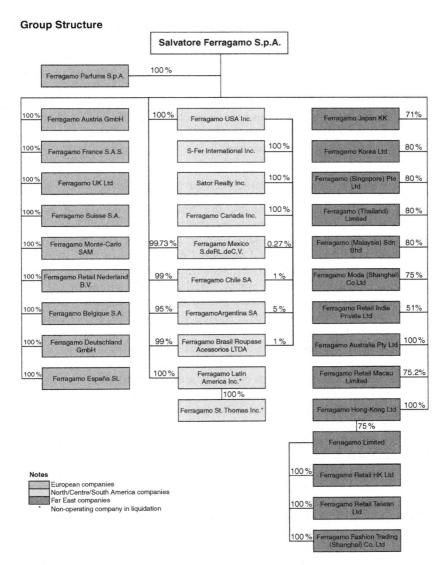

Fig. 3.8 Structure of Salvatore Ferragamo group (*Source*: Salvatore Ferragamo annual report, 2014)

standardized approach reduces management complexity on a retailing level and enhances brand awareness and recognition in the minds of customers. Entering a Salvatore Ferragamo store in Milan would not be so different from walking into a store in Tokyo or London. Such standardization is possible because the group directly operates 58 % of the stores, and more than 62 % of sales are generated from these directly operated stores. In addition, mono brand stores, including both retail and wholesale channels, represent the majority of the distribution network and play an important role in brand positioning.

CONCLUSION AND IMPLICATIONS

Salvatore Ferragamo was among the first to export Italian fashion products; he shaped the identity of the "Made in Italy" label as we know it today. It could be said that he pioneered the blending and balancing of craftsmanship and industrial production, as well as the use of evocative images related to "Italian taste" in order to communicate his firm's character. The concept of "Made in Italy" spread in the postwar period, during the so-called Italian economic miracle (Paulicelli, 2014). Far from being uniquely related to manufacturing origins, the expression "Made in Italy" first communicates the *taste* and *style* that historically can be traced back to the Renaissance period, particularly to Florence. Looking more specifically to the fashion industry, the term has become widely associated with creativity and craftsmanship.

All these iconic elements—the *Italian taste*, the screen "stars," the Italian craft tradition and creativeness, and even the Renaissance iconography—are traceable in the Salvatore Ferragamo brand and have been consciously leveraged by its founder and family until the present. Salvatore Ferragamo has led the way in shaping the meaning of "Made in Italy" in the fashion industry during its 88 years of history. As with many family business companies, the brand started as a workshop and has since become a global player in its industry, all while maintaining familial entrepreneurship at the heart of its organizational structure and identity.

More specifically, Salvatore Ferragamo has transitioned from a single-product to a multi-category company, from a product-oriented brand to a retail–oriented brand, and from a family business company to a publicly traded one. Its corporate brand strategy focuses on brand heritage as an intrinsic facet of its value proposition and an asset of worldwide brand positioning. The brand heritage of Salvatore Ferragamo—a dimension composed by functional and symbolic assets—constitutes the "fil rouge" of the brand's value proposition, the pillar of its consistency and continuity, and the pivot on which the brand has positioned itself to face the evolution of time. Within this evolutionary process, the figure of Salvatore Ferragamo assumes a mythical and narrative dimension, with Ferragamo's family currently assuming the role of brand guardian over time. An example for all could be identified in the firm's decision to bring forward the founder's signature as brand lettering.

Leveraging brand heritage during the two key development trajectories of the firm—brand extension and internationalization—is only possible due to a centralized decision process and a shared group organizational model for various product categories and markets.

The firm has been situated in an ongoing tension between tradition and innovation and has subsequently identified the founder and brand heritage as their compasses. They constitute strength and strategic assets in the structuring of brand awareness and brand consistency worldwide and over time. However, they may also constitute a challenge primarily in translating such strong assets into new dynamic communicative approaches.

Notes

1. In April 2016, Michele Norsa announced the will to exit the Ferragamo Group by the end of the year.
2. In ancient Roman religion and myth, Vulcan was the god of metalworking and the forge. Vulcan was considered the manufacturer of art, arms, iron, and jewelry.
3. The Salvatore Ferragamo Museum is one of the 48 associates of Museimpresa, the Italian association of corporate museums and archives. The association enumerates several categories—such as Food, Design, Fashion, Engines, Economy and Society, Research, and Innovation—of historical companies that have decided to invest in the development of their industrial heritage.

References

Aaker, D. A. (2004). Leveraging the corporate brand. *California Management Review, 46*(3), 6–18. doi:10.2307/41166218

Bhat, S., & Reddy, S. K. (1998). Symbolic and functional positioning of brands. *Journal of Consumer Marketing, 15*(1), 32–43. doi:10.1108/07363769810202664

Ciucchi, S. (n.d.). *Salvatore Ferragamo*. [PowerPoint Presentation].

Del Río, B. A., Vazquez, R., & Iglesias, V. (2001). The effects of brand associations on consumer response. *Journal of Consumer Marketing, 18*(5), 410–425. doi:10.1108/07363760110398808

Ferragamo, S. (1957). *Shoemaker of dreams. The autobiography of Salvatore Ferragamo*. London: George G. Harrap & Co.

Ferragamo, S. (2014). Bilancio di Sostenibilità 2014. Retrieved from https://www.enel.com/it-it/Documents/FinancialReports/report2014/enel_bilan cio_sostenibilita_2014.pdf

Floch, J. M. (1990). *Sémiotique: marketing et communication. Sous Les Signes, Les Stratégies*. Paris: PUF.

Keller, K. L. (1993). Conceptualizing, measuring, and managing customer-based brand equity. *Journal of Marketing, 57*(1), 1–22. doi:10.2307/1252054

Nissley, N., & Casey, A. (2002). The politics of the exhibition: viewing corporate museums through the paradigmatic lens of organizational memory. *British Journal of Management, 13(S2)*, S35–S45. doi:10.1111/1467-8551.13.s2.4

Paulicelli, E. (2014). Fashion: the cultural economy of made in Italy. *Fashion Practice, 6(2)*, 155–174.

Ricci, S., Morozzi, C., Ferragamo, W., & Kung, S. (2009). *Salvatore Ferragamo evolving legend 1928–2008*. Milan: Skira.

Salvatore Ferragamo Group. (2010). Annual report. Retrieved from http://group.ferragamo.com/wps/wcm/connect/e7fce6a8-faac-41fe-ba80-b2ad2a5b9fc4/Consolidated+Annual+Report+2010.pdf?MOD= AJPERES&CACHEID=e7fce6a8-faac-41fe-ba80-b2ad2a5b9fc4

Salvatore Ferragamo Group. (2011). Annual report. Retrieved from http://group.ferragamo.com/wps/wcm/connect/1a12078e-4da3-4009-af60-3c2391f1c983/Separate+Annual+Report+2011.pdf?MOD= AJPERES&CACHEID=1a12078e-4da3-4009-af60-3c2391f1c983

Salvatore Ferragamo Group. (2012). Annual report. Retrieved from http://group.ferragamo.com/wps/wcm/connect/66d4279f-cfcd-42c9-b4ca-23d7736c469f/Consolidated+Annual+Report+2012.pdf?MOD=AJPERES

Salvatore Ferragamo Group. (2013). Annual report. Retrieved from http://group.ferragamo.com/wps/wcm/connect/43f89b07-6f9f-46a8-bcd0-37dff9c4c402/Separate+Annual+Report+2013.pdf?MOD=AJPERES

Salvatore Ferragamo Group. (2014). Annual report. Retrieved from http://group.ferragamo.com/wps/wcm/connect/9ba067c7-e287-4ba7-971d-4a4acc505341/Annual+Report+as+at+31+December+2014.pdf?MOD= AJPERES&CACHEID=9ba067c7-e287-4ba7-971d-4a4acc505341

Salvatore Ferragamo Museum. (n.d.) Salvatore Ferragamo museum archive. Retrieved from http://www.ferragamo.com/museo/en/usa/

Salvatore Ferragamo website. (2015). Company website. Retrieved from http://www.ferragamo.com

Urde, M., Greyser, S. A., & Balmer, J. M. T. (2007). Corporate brands with a heritage. *Journal of Brand Management, 15*(1), 4–19. doi:10.1057/palgrave.bm.2550106

Maria Carmela Ostillio is Director and Core Faculty Member of the Brand Academy at SDA Bocconi School of Management, Milan, where she teaches Brand Management at master level. Before achieving a MBA degree, she worked for some companies in service-industry and distribution sector; then she has been cooperating with various consultant companies well known in the field of strategic management and marketing. Maria Carmela Ostillio has published papers on Marketing and Corporate Communications and Brand Management, Direct & Interactive Marketing, Marketing One to One, Customer Database and Marketing Information Systems.

Sarah Ghaddar is Research Fellow at SDA Bocconi School of Management. She gained professional experience in the Marketing Department of multinational companies and SMEs, with a focus on Digital Marketing, Search Engine Optimization Marketing and consumer behavior. Her research interests lie in the field of consumer behavior, customer centricity, value co-creation and digital marketing.

CHAPTER 4

Tod's: A Global Multi-Brand Company with a Taste of Tradition

Maria Carmela Ostillio and Sarah Ghaddar

Abstract As with many other Italian companies, the Tod's Group began as a family business and has since evolved into a global fashion player boasting a portfolio of four brands (Tod's, Hogan, Fay, and Roger Vivier). The group operates in 37 countries and yields a total sales revenue of €965.5 million as of 2014, approximately 70 % of which has been generated from exports. The Tod's Group adopts a double management approach: (i) a vertical strategic decision-making process in the upstream to ensure the entire group achieves cost and operation efficiency and (ii) a horizontal operating process in the downstream to guarantee a diversified identity of brands in terms of design, marketing, and retail management. The group employs a hybrid branding strategy, wherein the core brand Tod's utilizes a corporate dominant strategy while the other brands (Fay, Hogan, and Roger Vivier) prefer brand dominant strategies. Tod's, the group's core brand, currently leads the group's global markets, representing approximately 60 % of overall sales in

M.C. Ostillio (✉)
SDA Bocconi School of Management, Milan, Italy

S. Ghaddar
Department of Marketing – Claudio Dematté Research, SDA Bocconi School of Management, Milan, Italy

© The Author(s) 2017
B. Jin, E. Cedrola (eds.), *Fashion Branding and Communication*,
Palgrave Studies in Practice: Global Fashion Brand Management,
DOI 10.1057/978-1-137-52343-3_4

101

2014 and 70 % of its stores worldwide. This chapter explains the group's unique approach to brand communication and commitment to corporate social responsibility, particularly in terms of local communities, the environment, and the welfare of its stakeholders and employees.

Keywords Brand portfolio strategy · Multi-brand company · Retail store · Corporate social responsibility

INTRODUCTION

Although some consumers might assume Tod's to be either a British or American brand due to its Anglophone name, the Tod's Group actually traces its roots to Italy (Seabrook, 2004). The group's headquarters is located in Casette D'Ete (Sant'Elpidio a Mare), a small town in the Marche region of Italy, where the Della Valle family's original business began. Today, the group operates four proprietary brands—Tod's, Hogan, Fay, and Roger Vivier—and remains actively involved in the creation, production, and distribution of shoes, leather goods, and accessories. As of 2014, the group registered a sales revenue of €965.5 million, about 70 % of which was generated from exports.

With its articulated brand portfolio, the Tod's Group covers a broad range of market segments, from affordable products to luxury brands. The group has created a clear identity for each brand in its portfolio and thereby enhanced each brand's awareness and image. The core brand Tod's leads the group in global markets, representing approximately 60 % of overall sales in 2014 and 70 % of its stores worldwide. Among its 325 mono-brand stores, Tod's has 216 stores, including 139 directly operated stores (DOS) and 77 franchising stores. In the midst of international promotion, Tod's has structured its identity in terms of *Italian style* and *philosophy*, leveraging the *Made in Italy* label, Italian traditional craftsmanship, and the so-called *Italian way-of-life*, in order to differentiate itself at the global level. The group has actively engaged in local and national territory, adopting its Italian-ness as a core value proposition.

This chapter will focus on the group's history, overview, recent market outcomes, brand portfolio strategy (particularly on that of Tod's as the pillar brand), and corporate social responsibility (CSR) approach. The discussion of the latter will highlight the group's commitment to its local territory and human resources management as a distinctive part of its value proposition and corporate philosophy.

This case was developed based on the authors' visits to the Tod's Group's headquarters in May of 2015, along with several interviews involving a wide spectrum of employees and collaborators ranging from top management to manufacturing workforce. Secondary data from the company's annual reports, trade and academic journals, books, articles, websites, and other media sources in English and in Italian were also analyzed.

BRIEF HISTORY OF THE TOD'S GROUP

The Tod's Group began in the early 1900s when a gentleman named Filippo Della Valle founded a small, family-run footwear workshop in the small town of Casette D'Ete in Italy's Marche region. After the founder's death in the 1940s, the family business fell into the hands of his son Dorino Della Valle until the 1970s, after which his first son Diego Della Valle obtained the office. Although no official story explains the brand's name, it is said that Diego Della Valle sought an English name that could be easily pronounced and remembered. The decision was made on "Tod," a name he discovered by flipping through the telephone directory.

Under Dorino Della Valle's leadership in the 1960s, the original workshop became a shoe factory known as the "Della Valle Shoe Factory" located in the Marche region's historic footwear district. Starting in the mid-1970s, the company engaged in several partnerships and produced shoes for established fashion firms, such as Lacroix, Krizia, Ferré, and Versace, in addition to creating, producing, and distributing the Della Valle shoes line.

During this period, the company experienced a major transition from its status as a family business to an industrial company. Through marketing, the brand gained increased exposure at the national and international levels. The company also initiated brand portfolio extensions and a product line expansion. Under the guidance of Diego Della Valle, the group's current president and CEO, the company has gradually become the global fashion player it is today.

In 1998, the group established its headquarters at Casette D'Ete, a small town in the Marche region in which the family business first started.

Fig. 4.1   Tod's headquarter (*Source*: Tod's Group archive.) *Note*: Tod's Group website (2015)

The headquarters, located on "Filippo Della Valle Road," is a contemporary white marble building with large windowed facades nestled in the Marche Hills (Fig. 4.1). The building is adorned with several pieces of contemporary art, and the structure as a whole occupies a surface of 250,000 square meters, overlooking 65,000 square meters of greenery.

The company continues to invest in the renovation and development of its headquarters, which offers several free-of-charge services for the employees such as a kindergarten, fitness center, free canteen, and video library. Such benefits are uncommon among Italian companies. Next to the headquarters is a company-owned shoe factory, one of the largest luxury shoe factories in the world (Seabrook, 2004) and the largest production center for luxury footwear in Italy.

The group was listed on the Milan Stock Exchange in 2000, with a minimum price of €22 per share. The Della Valle family still plays a key role within the organizational structure, with Diego Della Valle serving as Chairman and Andrea Della Valle serving as Vice-Chairman and President of the Hogan brand. Beyond these formal roles, the family consistently facilitates daily work activities, not only in the strategic decision-making process, but also in the entire value chain process.

COMPANY OVERVIEW

TOD'S S.p.A. is the parent company that manages the group's organizational structure and the entire value chain from suppliers to customers. Currently, the group consists of the parent company and its 46 subsidiaries (9 direct subsidiaries and 37 indirect subsidiaries).[1] The subsidiary network comprises the following: companies that manage directly operated stores (DOS); companies located in strategic geographic markets that manage product distribution and brand promotion in the USA, Germany, France, Great Britain, Spain, Hong Kong, Korea, and the Far East; one company for services; and two production companies located in East Europe.

In 2014, the group's workforce totaled 4,297 employees: 50 executives, 2,981 white-collar workers, and 1,266 blue-collar workers. In the past 5 years, the workforce has increased by 34.5 % (1,103 more employees in 2014 than in 2010). The group is active in 37 countries, with a particularly strong presence in Europe and Greater China.

Sales and Market Share

Table 4.1 shows the group's financial statement for the past five years (2010–2014). As indicated, there have been increases in exports from 46 % to 67.8 %, the number of DOS from 230 to 325, and the number of employees from 3194 to 4297. Sales through the DOS totaled €616 million as of December 31, 2014, and represented 63.8 % of the total revenue, the rest coming from the franchise and independent stores (Table 4.2).

Within the brand portfolio, Tod's sales revenue represents 58.9 % of the total, followed by Hogan (22.0 %), Roger Vivier (13.1 %), and Fay (5.9 %) (Table 4.3). In terms of product category, shoes represent 77 % of total sales revenue, while leather goods and accessories account for 16.1 % and apparel accounts for 6.8 % (Table 4.4).

As shown in Table 4.5, Italy contributes 32.2 % of overall sales revenues. The rest of Europe—particularly Germany, the United Kingdom, and Spain—contributes 22.9 %. The greater China (which includes China, Hong Kong, Macao and Taiwan) region was the group's first foreign market and accounted for 23.4 % of sales revenues in 2014. The group's sales in the Americas (including United States and Brazil, with a major presence in the United States) totaled €87.3 million, corresponding to 9 % of the total revenue. Among the remaining 12.5 % of total sales, Japan and Korea also play an important role in number of DOS.

Table 4.1   Tod's Group's financial statement, 2010–2014

	2014	2013	2012	2011	2010
Total Sales Revenues (€million)	965.5	967.5	963.1	893.6	787.5
EBITDA (€million)	193.5 (20.0 % of sales revenues)	236.3 (24.4 % of sales revenues)	250.2 (25.9 % of sales revenues)	232.4 (26.0 % of sales revenues)	193.1 (24.5 % of sales revenues)
Net profits (€million)	96.8	134	145.7	135.7	110.8
Export share	67.8 %	66.6 %	60.1 %	49.7 %	46.0 %
Number of employees in the group	4,297	4,144	3,878	3,549	3,194
Number of mono-brand stores	325	303	271	246	230
Number of directly operated stores among mono-brand stores	232	219	193	176	159

EBITDA: Earnings Before Interest, Taxes, Depreciation, and Amortization
Note: Elaborated by the authors with data published on Tod's annual report 2010–2014

Table 4.2   Tod's Group's sales revenues by distribution network, 2010–2014 (€million)

	2014	2013	2012	2011	2010
Total Sales Revenues	965.5 (100 %)	967.5 (100 %)	963.1 (100 %)	893.6 (100 %)	787.5 (100 %)
Directly Operated Stores	616.0 (63.8 %)	617.7 (63.8 %)	574.1 (59.6 %)	474.3 (53.1 %)	403.8 (51.3 %)
Wholesale	349.5 (36.2 %)	349.8 (36.2 %)	389.0 (40.4 %)	419.3 (46.9 %)	383.7 (48.7 %)

Note: Elaborated by the authors with data published on Tod's annual report 2010–2014

Production and Distribution

With regard to production, there are six proprietary manufacturing plants located in Italy (four in the Marche region and two in the Tuscany region), along with two indirectly controlled production companies in Albany and Hungary. Additionally, the group has established a long-term relationship with small workshops for outsourcing. The manufacturing process differs among the many products and brands. For instance, most

Table 4.3   Tod's Group's sales revenues by brand, 2010–2014 (€million)[a]

	2014	2013	2012	2011	2010
Total Sales Revenues	965.5	967.5	963.1	893.6	787.5
	(100 %)	(100 %)	(100 %)	(100 %)	(100 %)
Tod's	568.0	578.1	569.7	487.5	407.0
	(58.9 %)	(59.7 %)	(59.2 %)	(54.6 %)	(51.7 %)
Hogan	212.3	217.0	243.4	280.9	268.3
	(22 %)	(22.4 %)	(25.3 %)	(31.4 %)	(34.1 %)
Fay	57.3	57.6	74.5	87.8	89.7
	(5.9 %)	(6 %)	(7.7 %)	(9.8 %)	(11.4 %)
Roger Vivier	126.9	113.7	74.5	36.5	21.7
	(13.1 %)	(11.8 %)	(7.7 %)	(4.1 %)	(2.7 %)

Note: Elaborated by the authors with data published on Tod's annual report 2010–2014
[a]The total sales and corresponding percent may be just a little bit less than 100 % because of rounding. This happened because their original annual reports were in €million.

Table 4.4   Tod's Group's sales revenues by product category, 2010–2014 (€million)

	2014	2013	2012	2011	2010
Total Sales	965.5	967.5	963.1	893.6	787.5
Revenues	(100 %)	(100 %)	(100 %)	(100 %)	(100 %)
Shoes	743.5	739.7	710.4	646.5	564.6
	(77 %)	(76.5 %)	(73.7 %)	(72.3 %)	(71.7 %)
Leather Goods	155.6	160.9	165.5	144.9	123.2
	(16.1 %)	(16.6 %)	(17.2 %)	(16.2 %)	(15.6 %)
Apparel	65.4	65.8	86.2	101.6	99.1
	(6.8 %)	(6.8 %)	(9 %)	(11.4 %)	(12.6 %)
Other	1.0 (0.1 %)	1.1 (0.1 %)	1.0 (0.1 %)	0.6 (0.1 %)	0.6 (0.1 %)

Note: Elaborated by the authors with data published on Tod's annual report 2010–2014

production plants reside across different regions in central Italy: shoes manufacturing in Marche and Abruzzo and leather goods in Tuscany. Meanwhile, certain manufacturing phases for Hogan and Fay are off-shored in Eastern Europe.

The group's distribution structure mainly relies on three channels: DOS, franchised retail outlets, and a series of independent multi-brand stores. Among the 325 mono-brand stores, 232 are DOS while 93 are

Table 4.5   Tod's Group's sales revenues by geographic regions, 2010–2014 (€million)

	2014	2013	2012	2011	2010
Total Sales Revenues	965.5	967.5	963.1	893.6	787.5
	(100 %)	(100 %)	(100 %)	(100 %)	(100 %)
Italy	311.1	323.0	383.9	449.3	425.7
	(32.2 %)	(33.4 %)	(39.9 %)	(50.3 %)	(54 %)
Greater China	225.7	237.5	195.9	/	/
	(23.4 %)	(24.5 %)	(20.3 %)		
Europe (excluding Italy)	221.3	207.8	200.3	182.0	163.7
	(22.9 %)	(21.5 %)	(20.8 %)	(20.4 %)	(20.8 %)
North America	/	/	/	62.4	53.4
				(6.9 %)	(6.8 %)
Rest of the World	120.1	108.9	101.4	199.9	144.7
	(12.5 %)	(11.3 %)	(10.5 %)	(22.4 %)[a]	(18.4 %)[a]
Americas	87.3	90.3	81.6	/	/
	(9 %)	(9.3 %)	(8.5 %)		

[a]Asia and rest of the world
Note: Elaborated by the authors with data published on Tod's annual report 2010–2014

franchised stores. Franchising has served as the primary channel of entry into new markets, although it is rarely seen in the domestic market.

Several subsidiary companies, either directly or indirectly held by the group, manage retail distribution through the DOS network and oversee marketing with promotions and public relations. The group focuses on the development of DOS and franchising networks, since these channels play an important role in shaping each brand's identity. From 2010 to 2014, there was a 41.3 % increase in the number of mono-brand stores (increase of 45.9 % in DOS and 31.0 % in franchised stores). Depending on market situations, the group has also at times utilized multi-brand stores as channels by which to enter new markets.

Organization

The group's structure comprises a vertical decision-making process in the upstream and a horizontal operating process in the downstream. The upstream strategic decision-making is centralized, while brands in the downstream are managed separately in terms of design, marketing, and retail management. The company's headquarters vertically manages the strategic decision-making processes of each product, brand, and geographic market. In this way, the parent company exercises control over a large degree of the group's activity, from the design process to the production and distribution processes. For example, the headquarters oversees key stages of the manufacturing process, such as raw materials purchase, supervision of production phases, and quality control for finished products. This centralized approach assures consistent adherence to the group's vision across different geographical markets and brands, which in turn allows for higher levels of cost and operational efficiency. At the same time, the downstream approach ensures a diversified identity for each brand in the portfolio.

Brand Portfolio Strategy

The brand portfolio strategies of the Tod's Group have focused on brand acquisition, product-line extension to small leather goods and travel goods, and extension into completely new product categories such as apparel. The Tod's Group's brand portfolio extension began in the 1980s under Diego Della Valle's leadership. Since Tod's creation in the early 1980s, Hogan, Fay, and Roger Vivier have also been added to the portfolio. The group acquired Hogan from Dorint for €93 million and Fay from Paflux for €61.9 million in 2001.[2] In 2007, Diego Della Valle began the acquisition process of Elsa Schiaparelli, a brand founded in 1935 by an Italian designer and positioned in *the prêt-à-porter segment*.[3] The group acquired its trademark and brand archive before re-launching it in 2012. Finally, the group acquired Roger Vivier in 2015.

Each brand maintains a specific identity in relation to its target market segment. The core product category of all brands in the portfolio, with the exception of Fay, is footwear and leather goods, for both men and women. Fay's main product offering is apparel. The group's brand portfolio aims to cover a wide range of market segments, from more affordable brands such as Hogan and Fay to high-end luxury segments such as Roger Vivier (Fig. 4.2). Within the brand portfolio, Tod's plays the role of a pioneer in the global market, followed by Roger Vivier. Hogan and Fay are currently popular in the domestic market but struggle internationally. Below is a summary of the four brands in the portfolio.

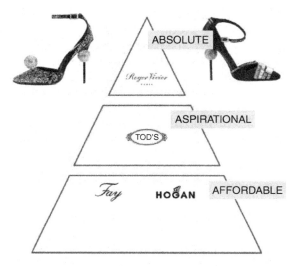

Fig. 4.2 Tod's Group's Brand Portfolio (*Note*: Tod's Group (2015); Retrieved from https://www.todsgroup.com)

Tod's

Tod's, as the main brand of the group, was launched in the early 1980s. It first featured a footwear line and has since added leather goods in the late 1990s and a ready-to-wear collection in recent years. Compared to the group's other brands, Tod's currently operates in a more mature phase of its internationalization process and maintains strong global brand awareness. Tod's is positioned in the portfolio's medium-high-level segment, serving as an "aspirational" brand. It emphasizes tradition, high quality, and modernity by leveraging its *Made in Italy* craftsmanship and its so-called *Italian way-of-life*. The brand's proposition and values are enhanced by such marketing efforts, which also include testimonials of people who embody the Italian lifestyle. Additionally, since the early 2000s, Tod's has partnered with Ferrari S.p.A., one of the most well-known Italian brands in the world and one that closely identifies with the Made-in-Italy concept. The partnership allows Ferrari and Tod's to collaborate and produce limited edition products.

The footwear line still represents Tod's core business and market share in terms of product offering. In recent years, Tod's has engaged in a brand extension process through the introduction of complementary product lines, such as apparel and accessories. The Gommino moccasin, characterized by 133 rubber pebbles on the sole, has been Tod's iconic product since 1978. The name is derived from the Italian word "gomma," which means rubber.

Hogan

Launched in 1986, Hogan is positioned at the base of the pyramid, with lower price positioning accounting for 22 % of the overall revenue (as stated in the 2014 annual report). While other brands in the group specialize mostly in specific product categories, Hogan offers a wide range of products, from footwear and leather goods to accessories and apparel. Hogan also targets a broad consumer base consisting of women, men, and children, mainly buyers in the age group of 20–55. However, its brand proposition primarily addresses younger consumers and communicates innovation and trendiness, championing the "new luxury" lifestyle.

Despite the group's Made-in-Italy heritage, part of Hogan's manufacturing process is conducted in Eastern Europe due to cost reduction policies. The brand is situated in an initial phase of the internationalization and brand awareness process. Hogan operates mostly in the domestic market, with 23 of 40 mono-brand stores managed by the brand. The remaining stores are located in Europe (five stores), China (seven stores) and the Middle East (five stores, three of which are in the Persian Gulf), as of January 2016. Hogan's brand expansion strategy has shown the most progress in China, where it registered a double-digit sales growth rates in 2015 compared to the first nine months of the previous year.

In terms of product portfolio, footwear serves as Hogan's core business, comprising most of its sales revenue despite the brand's product differentiation strategy. Casual shoes such as "Traditional" and "Interactive" continue to be Hogan's best-selling products (Fig. 4.3). Interactive, in particular, makes up a major share of the sales volume of Hogan in Italy. The Interactive model's strong association with the Hogan brand has posed a challenge since it seeks to offer a total look to consumers. One interviewee at Tod's addressed that the brand struggled to moderate the sales of Hogan Interactive, imposing a constraint to clients' order. There was a time when the Interactive could not exceed 50 % of the whole order.

Fig. 4.3 Hogan's iconic products—Traditional (*left*) and Interactive (*right*) (*Note*: Hogan website; Retrieved from www.hogan.com)

Fay

Fay entered the brand portfolio in the late 1980s. It represented the group's first effort in a brand portfolio expansion strategy aimed at broadening its offering through a complementary product-line. Within the brand portfolio, Fay—along with Hogan—is located at the base of the pyramid with more affordable price positioning. It offers a wide range of casual wear, including men's, women's, and junior collections. The products are designed in classic styles suitable for daily life. Fay's sales revenue corresponds to €57.3 million, which accounts for 5.9 % of the group's overall revenue. It operates predominantly in the domestic market primarily through wholesalers; currently, the 20 mono-brand stores are all located in Italy, except for one in Madrid, Spain.

Roger Vivier

Roger Vivier inherited its name from its creator, who is often credited with the invention of the "stiletto" heel in the 1950s. Roger Vivier, a French fashion designer who specialized in shoes, earned the nickname "the Fabergé of footwear." The House Fabergé is a historical jewelry brand associated with high quality and luxury. After Vivier's death in 1998, the Della Valle family acquired the brand in 2001 to maintain brand identity and the designer's artistic heritage and tradition, while also implementing a product-line expansion. For instance, management in recent years has given new emphasis to certain iconic products, such as the Pilgrim pumps (Fig. 4.4). The brand was finally acquired by the Tod's Group in 2015 at €415 million (plus €20 million for the acquisition of Roger Vivier's historical flagship store in Paris).[4] The

Fig. 4.4 Roger Vivier's iconic product—Pilgrim pumps (*Source*: Tod's Group archive (2015))

recent acquisition process of Roger Vivier reflects the group's three main objectives: to remove license uncertainty, exercise full control of long-term planning for Roger Vivier with the aim of improving sales revenue, and to increase brand value and its long-term growth potential.

Currently, Roger Vivier has an EBITDA (Earnings Before Interest, Taxes, Depreciation, and Amortization) margin higher than the group's average even after the royalty payment. In terms of brand identity and proposition, Roger Vivier is one of the most exclusive and luxurious brands in the group's portfolio, with a product offering of shoes, handbags, small leather goods, sunglasses, and jewelry. With respect to the original brand identity, the current brand position aims to recreate a timeless Parisian elegance, sophistication, and extravagance.

Roger Vivier possesses an exclusive distribution network, with presence in key luxury cities around the globe. In line with the group's policy, the brand maintains a direct distribution system: 31 DOS and 4 franchised stores as of September 30, 2015. The stores carry a unique combination of modern and vintage elements. Compared to the rest of the portfolio, Roger Vivier has weak influence in the domestic market but a strong presence in the Asia-Pacific.

TOD'S BRAND COMMUNICATION VIA STORYTELLING AND RETAIL NETWORK

Tod's plays a central role in the brand portfolio, not only in terms of market share, but also in terms of representing the group's main values and business strategies. Tod's leads the group's internationalization

Fig. 4.5 Tod's storytelling through a book "*Italian Portraits*" (*Source*: Tod's Group archive (2015))

process and functions as its flagship in the domestic market, making way for other brands in the portfolio.

Instead of relying only on traditional marketing channels such as fashion magazines, Tod's has taken two approaches: (i) a brand storytelling approach through books and videos to highlight Tod's philosophy and (ii) a retail store network. The Tod's group has recently published four books internationally, using the power of images to communicate its brand identity and philosophy, as exemplified by Figs. 4.5 and 4.6.

Tod's Brand Values Communicated Through Storytelling

Italian Touch (2009) and *Italian Portraits* (2012) feature several testimonials of Italians, depicted in their everyday lives, who celebrate the *Italian aesthetic* and "*la dolce vita.*" The "everyday life" is immortalized

Fig. 4.6 Tod's storytelling through a book "*Italian Touch*" (*Source*: Tod's Group archive (2015))

through the presence of historic palaces and Italian countryside in the background. The timeless, classic style of the book signifies Tod's brand identity reaching beyond passing fads.

The other two are sponsored books, celebrating the Italian style through historical portraits of two global icons, Princess Diana and Jacqueline Kennedy. *Timeless icons*, published in 2013, presents Princess Diana's everyday life, wearing iconic Tod's products such as the Gommino shoes and the D-bag—the bag she made popular worldwide. *Un mito nel mito* (a myth in the myth) features Jacqueline Kennedy during her vacation in the Island of Capri in the early 1970s (Fig. 4.7). These last two books also illustrate the timeless, classic style of Tod's that still comes across as fashionable under today's standards.

Tod's Brand Identity Communicated Through Retail Stores

In addition to Tod's storytelling approach, the group relies on its retail store network for marketing communications. This network represents a huge investment for the group and plays a key role in shaping the brand's identity. The physical stores have become ideal communication channels for engaging customers with *lifestyle* experiences. The group has recently launched a new retail concept called the DEV boutiques in Italy, which features all brands in the portfolio within a single store (Roger Vivier has not yet been included). Since the mid-2000s, 19 DEV boutiques have opened, mostly in the northern and center regions of Italy where the group maintains its largest market share in the domestic market.

Fig. 4.7 Tod's storytelling through a book "*Un mito nel mito*" (*Source*: Tod's Group archive (2015))

One noticeable initiative that reinforces the brand's Italian heritage and luxury image is the launch of a new clothing collection for men, known as the J.P. Tod's Sartorial collection. It was launched in 2014 and was only available at selected boutiques in luxury locations, such as Paris, Tokyo, Shanghai, Beverly Hills, and Milan. Another initiative called "the Gommino Club" also aimed to strengthen brand image through iconic Gommino driving shoes that customers could customize in terms of leather, laces, and colors. Tod's also presents a live demonstration of shoe manufacturing by Italian artisans in its boutiques, allowing customers to experience the manufacturing process of Tod's iconic products.

Tod's Initiatives on Corporate Social Responsibility

Corporate Social Responsibility (CSR) applies to situations in which a company reaches beyond compliance and engages in actions that appear to further some social good, beyond the interests of the firm and that which is required by law (McWilliams & Siegel, 2001). CSR is a multi-dimensional concept consisting of different ethical responsibilities that a company should consider in business operations (Nasrullah & Rahim, 2014), such as environmental, social, economic, stakeholder, and voluntariness dimensions (Dahlsurd, 2008).

First, the environmental dimension accounts for the company's role in contributing to a cleaner environment through its business operations (World Business Council for Sustainable Development, 1999). The social dimension describes the relationship between business and society—in other words, how a business integrates social concerns into its operations. The economic dimension represents the socio-economic or financial aspects of business operations. The stakeholder dimension reflects how a business interacts with stakeholders such as employees, suppliers, customers, and communities. Lastly, the voluntariness dimension refers to actions not prescribed by law but based on ethical values (Dahlsurd, 2008).

The Tod's Group has actively incorporated CSR values into their business operations, embracing several dimensions of CSR (stakeholder, environmental, and social) as detailed below.

Stakeholder Dimension—Investing in Human Capital

The company's investment in human capital has continued for decades. The practices of CSR on improving the working environment for employees can take three forms: the provision of complementary services within the workplace, a welfare system, and a low turnover rate. The employee welfare system of the Tod's Group is among the most modern systems of its kind in Italy, providing its employees with a health insurance policy that can be extended to family members in cases of serious illness. The company covers the full cost of textbooks for its employees' school-aged children up through university. Furthermore, the headquarters offers exceptional perks and facilities such as a kindergarten, fitness center, free canteen, small library, and video library—facilities not commonly seen in other Italian companies.

Although the industry is characterized by a high turnover rate, the Tod's Group boasts a relatively low turnover rate in recent years. Also, most employees, being locals, have built their careers within the group. It is typical to find many employees from two or even three generations of the same family working in the company's manufacturing department.

Two noteworthy initiatives can be identified with regard to employee training. The first is a training program launched in 2014 called "*Fabbrica del Talento*" (Talent Factory). It provides twenty young people with six months of training focused on specific skills related to the manufacturing process. Afterward, the group hires about 70 % of the trainees. The program is meant to preserve key manual steps that require craftsmanship within the manufacturing process. Because of the aging workforce and rapid technological development, the transfer of manufacturing knowledge and skills to upcoming generations has become a pressing issue.

The second noteworthy initiative is tied to the role of stores—especially mono-brand stores—in shaping the relationship between brand and customer. A project launched in 2014 involves the store managers of the group's distribution network.

> The store staff represents the final step of the value chain. Everything starts from an idea, followed by the design process, the fashion collection, communication and advertising, all finally ending with the shopping experience. A firm may have planned these phases carefully, but at the end of the cycle, a customer can encounter a selling assistant in a bad mood, which destroys the job of thousands of people in a few seconds. A bad shopping experience could really destroy a brand. (Interview with Maria Cristina Modenesi, Head of Corporate Communication, 2015)

To address this, store managers spend a week touring the Milan office, where Tod's marketing department and PR office are located, as well as its headquarters and production sites. The group is aware of the importance of engaging its employees in the company's branding. Hence, the touring of the headquarters and production sites is often extended to employees working in the Milan offices as well.

Another project deals with the group's major foreign market: China. In 2014, Tod's initiated an employee exchange program between Italy and China. The program provided certain Chinese store managers, who were selected based on seniority and merit, with an opportunity to live in Italy for three months. With the support of two tutors, the employees received training on store management and Tod's corporate values, while familiarizing themselves with the Italian lifestyle and the concept of "made in Italy."

Social Dimension—Serving the Local Community

The second asset of CSR deals with service to the local community and its heritage. It comprises two different approaches: the preservation of the Della Valle family's values and of Italian artistic heritage. For the former, the group currently allocates 1 % of its net profit to charity projects involving local communities. For the latter, the group invests significant effort into the preservation of Italian artistic heritage, thereby promoting the group's brand identity and values.

The group has engaged in two large projects involving two Italian historic sites: Teatro alla Scala—the opera house in Milan—and the Colosseum in Rome. These initiatives fulfill the group's values of quality and Italianness by leveraging the *Made in Italy* concept, the *Italian life-style*, and various Italian traditional crafts. They began with the group's desire to protect and promote Italian culture, since doing so would associate the brand with Italian values and render it more competitive in the marketplace (Tod's group website, 2015).

In 2011, the group reached an agreement with the Italian Ministry of Cultural Affairs and the Rome Special Archaeological Service to invest a total of €25 million for restoration projects on the Colosseum. The first of three phases for the Colosseum's restoration started in 2014, focusing on the north and south façade and the installation of gates around the perimeter.

In 2011, the group became a founding member of the Teatro alla Scala Foundation. The group has supported art collections primarily in Milan, including the Contemporary Art Pavilion (Padiglione D'arte Contemporanea) (PAC). The PAC was founded in Milan in 1954 and often hosts global art exhibitions, attracting about 20,000 visitors per exhibition. The group utilizes PAC to launch its own collections, allowing them to associate their product lines with artistic values. The group's role as a founding member of the Teatro alla Scala Foundation has been highlighted in a video campaign called "*An Italian Dream*" that was launched in 2010 during Milan's fashion week. The video celebrated the preservation of Italian heritage through operas and ballets, while also explaining Tod's efforts to preserve artisanal phases within its manufacturing process for products such as the Gommino.

Environmental Dimension—Increasing Energy Efficiency

Finally, the group has recently demonstrated its commitment to the environment, both through its headquarters and its mono-brand stores. The group has analyzed its consumption of energy at the headquarters in order to initiate a program aimed at gradually reducing its ecological footprint. After monitoring its energy consumption, the group implemented an energy-saving program in 2014. The company has since incorporated alternative geothermal and solar energy sources to supply part of its needs and to improve air conditioning efficiency.

In alignment with recent European policies regarding energy efficiency,[5] the project also includes the construction of a new 10,500 square-meter building located near the group's headquarters that meets the requirements of "passive houses."[6] The structure is characterized by low energy consumption due to its insulation and recovery of rainwater and by its new LED lighting system. It also relies on solar and geothermal plants for heating and cooling. The same insulation method has also been recently applied to two manufacturing plants in Marche. Retail stores have adopted such improvements to energy efficiency as well, using LED technology to light interior spaces and sales displays and utilizing recycled furnishing to conserve wood.

SUMMARY AND DISCUSSIONS

Since its industrialization in the 1960s, the Tod's Group has evolved into a global fashion player while preserving its family business origins. It has established a successful global presence mainly due to its core and historic brand—Tod's—and its consistent branding strategies.

The group's brand portfolio strategy of four brands strives to achieve operational efficiency, to centralize strategic decision-making processes, and to share a significant portion of activities throughout the value-chain. Upstream and downstream processes characterize the organization's structure. The upstream process refers to the strategic decision-making process centralized within the Parent Company, its purposes being to guarantee consistency in business strategy, to achieve cost and time efficiency, and to create synergy among brands. The downstream process has been initiated recently to ensure differentiation among the operational activities of each brand. Each brand's operational unit oversees its design process, marketing, and PR activities in order to differentiate brand image and identity within the portfolio.

Through the brand portfolio strategy, the group strives to gain operational synergy when available. The process of cost and operational efficiency involves the sharing of key stages and service activities along the value chain. Furthermore, nearly every brand in the portfolio uses a centralized approach in its product line expansion. For instance, when brands that are strongly tied to a specific product line such as footwear (e.g., Tod's and Hogan) try to introduce an apparel line to become a lifestyle brand, such centralized procedures are applied. These brands use the know-how gained by brands whose main product offering is apparel (e.g., Fay).

Tod's is the group's flagship brand and plays a representative role by promoting the group and its values abroad. Tod's embodies the group's values as identified by the group's website (2015): *craftsmanship, made in Italy, handmade, and heritage.* In the minds of customers, however, these values are not as strongly linked to the rest of the portfolio. This is an intentional decision made by the group, since they operate different brands in different markets (Barwise & Robertson, 1992). This strategy points to a hybrid branding solution wherein a corporate dominant strategy is used for the core brand while a brand dominant strategy is preferred for other brands (Fay, Hogan, and Roger Vivier) (Aaker & Joachimsthaler, 2000; Keller, Busacca, & Ostillio, 2005). It allows the company to obtain different positioning for the brands in its portfolio (Riezebos, Kist, & Kootstra, 2003), which explains why the Tod's Group communicates different marketing strategies for each of its brands in the international market. For example, Tod's emphasizes the Italian lifestyle through 'made in Italy' or artisanal features. On the other hand, Roger Vivier draws associations with French style and values that are distinguished from Tod's.

Finally, one of the main value propositions of the group and its philosophy is found in the preservation of tradition. The Della Valle family still plays a prominent role in business operations and has shown undivided commitment and support for the local community. Such commitment is deeply tied to its family business and local heritage.

NOTES

1. As of December 31, 2014, 1 direct subsidiary and 4 indirect subsidiaries were not operative (Group Annual Report 2014, p. 12).
2. Tod's annual report 2001.
3. The brand has been acquired by DIEGO DELLA VALLE & C. SAPA, a Diego Della Valle's personal holding (MFFashion May 8, 2012 http://www.mffashion.com/it/archivio/2012/05/08/diego-della-valle-fa-rivi vere-il-mito-di-schiaparelli).
4. Source: TOD'S GROUP -ACQUISITION OF ROGER VIVIER BRAND November 2015, p. 5.
5. More specifically the European Directive "Nearly Zero Energy Buildings," which requires all new buildings to be nearly zero-energy by the end of 2020 (end of 2018 for the public buildings).

6. The term passive house (Passivhaus in German) refers to a rigorous, voluntary standard for energy efficiency in a building, reducing its ecological footprint. It results in ultra-low energy buildings that require little energy for space heating or cooling (Passive house, n.d.).

REFERENCES

Aaker, D. A., & Joachimsthaler, E. (2000). *Brand leadership*. New York: The Free Press.

Barwise, P., & Robertson, T. (1992). Brand portfolios. *European Management Journal, 10*(3), 277–285. doi:10.1016/0263-2373(92)90021-u

Dahlsurd, A. (2008). How corporate social responsibility is defined: an analysis of 37 definitions. *Corporate Social Responsibility and Environmental Management, 15*(1), 1–13. doi:10.1002/csr.132

Hogan website. (2016). Online store. Retrieved from http://www.hogan.com/en_us/

Keller, K. L., Busacca, B., & Ostillio, M. C. (2005). *La gestione del brand: strategie e sviluppo*. Milano, Italy: Egea.

McWilliams, A., & Siegel, D. (2001). Corporate social responsibility: a theory of the firm perspective. *The Academy of Management Review, 26*(1), 117–127. doi:10.2307/259398

Nasrullah, N. M., & Rahim, M. M. (2014). *CSR in private enterprises in developing countries: evidences from the ready-made garments industry in Bangladesh*. Cham, Switzerland: Springer International Publishing Switzerland.

Passive house. (n.d.). In *Wikipedia*. Retrieved from https://en.wikipedia.org/wiki/Passive_house

Riezebos, H. J., Kist, B., & Kootstra, G. (2003). *Brand management: a theoretical and practical approach*. Harlow: Financial Times Prentice Hall.

Seabrook, J. (2004, May). Shoe dreams. *The New Yorker*. Retrieved from http://www.newyorker.com/magazine/2004/05/10/shoe-dreams

Tod's Group. (2010). Annual report. Retrieved from https://www.todsgroup.com/en/financial-data/statements/

Tod's Group. (2011). Annual report. Retrieved from https://www.todsgroup.com/en/financial-data/statements/

Tod's Group. (2012). Annual report. Retrieved from https://www.todsgroup.com/en/financial-data/statements/

Tod's Group. (2013). Annual report. Retrieved from https://www.todsgroup.com/en/financial-data/statements/

Tod's Group. (2014). Annual report. Retrieved from https://www.todsgroup.com/en/financial-data/statements/

Tod's Group. (2015). Tod's Group: a global luxury player. [PowerPoint slides]. Retrieved from https://www.todsgroup.com/system/document_ens/478/original/Presentazione_RV_transaction.pdf

Tod's Group archive. (2015). Tod's presents. Retrieved from http://www.tods.com/en_us/tods-touch/presents/

Tod's Group website. (2015). Company website. Retrieved from https://www.todsgroup.com

World Business Council for Sustainable Development. (1999). Corporate social responsibility: Meeting changing expectations. Retrieved from http://www.wbcsd.org/pages/edocument/edocumentdetails.aspx?id=82

Maria Carmela Ostillio is Director and Core Faculty Member of the Brand Academy at SDA Bocconi School of Management, Milan, where she teaches Brand Management at master level. Before achieving a MBA degree, she worked for some companies in service-industry and distribution sector; then she has been cooperating with various consultant companies well known in the field of strategic management and marketing. Maria Carmela Ostillio has published papers on Marketing and Corporate Communications and Brand Management, Direct & Interactive Marketing, Marketing One to One, Customer Database and Marketing Information Systems.

Sarah Ghaddar is Research Fellow at SDA Bocconi School of Management. She gained professional experience in the Marketing Department of multinational companies and SMEs with a focus on Digital Marketing, Search Engine Optimization Marketing and consumer behavior. Her research interests lie in the field of consumer behavior, customer centricity, value co-creation and digital marketing.

CHAPTER 5

The Prada Trend: Brand Building at the Intersection of Design, Art, Technology, and Retail Experience

Stefania Masè and Ksenia Silchenko

Abstract Prada is one of the most successful Italian fashion businesses with unique design aesthetics and provocative counter-mainstream spirit. It is also one of a few companies in the global luxury industry that have chosen to remain independent from mergers with multinational conglomerates, establishing and following its own strategy based on distinction and management coherence. The Prada case is an exemplary depiction of how global recognition of a luxury brand stems from a combination of a constant search for differentiation and shrewd business decisions ensuring efficiency, functionality, and resistance through time. Direct control over retail, well-delineated and

S. Masè (✉)
Atlantic Pyrenees department, Pau-Bayonne University School of Management, University of Pau and the Adour Region, Pau, Nouvelle-Aquitaine, France

K. Silchenko
Department of Economics and Law, University of Macerata, Macerata, Italy

© The Author(s) 2017   125
B. Jin, E. Cedrola (eds.), *Fashion Branding and Communication*,
Palgrave Studies in Practice: Global Fashion Brand Management,
DOI 10.1057/978-1-137-52343-3_5

uniform brand portfolio with quest for aesthetic and cultural relevance, transcendence of pure commerce to the world of art, technology, architecture, and focus on consumer dialogue through retail experience—all these elements help Prada become one of the most ambitious and trendsetting global luxury brands of modern days.

Keywords Brand building strategy · Experiential marketing · Brand innovation · Flagship stores · Prada

INTRODUCTION

Prada is the flagship brand of Prada Group, one of a few companies in the global luxury industry not to have succumbed to the lure of binding together with luxury conglomerates such as LVMH, Richmond or Kering, making of its independence one of the cornerstones of its strategy (Bertelli, 2012). The Prada Group currently includes five distinct brands operating in luxury fashion (Prada, Miu Miu, Church's, Car Shoe) and fine foods (Marchesi, 1824) markets. The independence of the group secures to all brands a continuous and direct dialogue with the end customer, mainly through the lever of retail channel.

This case is an exemplary depiction of how global recognition of Prada as luxury brand resulted from a combination of a constant search for distinction and "anti-fashion" creative strategy with shrewd business decisions. Even in the utmost creative industries, such as luxury fashion, the brand building always needs to be supported by an appropriate business model that ensures efficiency, functionality, and resistance through time (Kapferer, 2008).

This case opens with the brief overview of the Prada Group's current structure and position, retail network, and sales figures. Further, its history will be outlined as four distinct stages corresponding to focal changes and strategic turns taken by the group. After a more detailed description of brand portfolio, the rest of the case will focus on the Prada brand, paying special attention to the role of design and innovation enabling brand building strategy. We will describe some of the tools creatively used by the brand to renew its dialogue continually with end consumers in support of brand equity, including the brand contact with the art world, the massive use of technological tools, and the management of the directly operated stores network, known as Prada Green Stores. Furthermore, we will discuss the exclusive Prada Epicenter, hybrid flagship/museum/creative hub retail spaces created by the brand as a result of the search for differentiation, innovation, and expression of brand essence.

Company Overview

With a turnover of approximately €3.5 billion and publicly listed in Hong Kong stock exchange since 2011, the Prada Group can be considered one of the most successful Italian luxury fashion businesses. The group is headed by two CEOs: Miuccia Prada and Patrizio Bertelli. Miuccia Prada is a granddaughter of the company's founder Mario Prada and a creative and provocative spirit behind Prada's unique brand personality. Patrizio Bertelli, on the other hand, is a strategic mind steering the company in its international expansion. A former owner of a leather goods company in Tuscany, he is also Miuccia's lifelong partner in business and in personal life. Together Miuccia Prada and Patrizio Bertelli are considered one of the most influential couples in the world (Betts, 2005).

The group today consists of five brands (Prada, Miu Miu, Church's, Car Shoe & Marchesi, 1824) in leather goods, ready-to-wear and made-to-measure clothing, accessories and fragrances, restaurants, and fine food sectors. In every category, Prada Group brands are synonymous with exclusivity, sophistication, creativity, and modernity, which lead to a creation of "fashionless fashion"—as Miuccia Prada and Patrizio Bertelli themselves define it (Prada, 2015).

One of Prada's key success factors in their international expansion strategy is the ability to exert firm control over the extent and the quality of the supply and distribution networks. Referred to as "the backbone of the international expansion strategy," the group's distribution network today covers 70 countries with 605 directly operated stores (Prada, 2015). Only in the past five years the number of directly operated stores has almost doubled and considerably extended its geography (see Table 5.1), providing another proof that fashion retailers are the most international types of companies (Moore, Doherty & Doyle, 2010). All of the locations are carefully chosen in order to embody the brand personality, while the displays and interiors are created in collaboration with the most acclaimed and vanguard designers and architects in the world (Ryan, 2007). As of 2015, 86 % of Prada Group's net revenues come from directly operated stores (Prada, 2015), with the major share

Table 5.1   Global distribution of the Prada Group directly operated stores

Year / Region	2015	2014	2013	2012	2011	2010
Italy	52	51	51	48	44	37
Europe	168	167	150	137	115	88
Middle East	20	17	16	11	2	0
Asia (excluding Japan)	184	175	157	130	115	99
Japan	73	70	72	66	65	56
Africa	1	4	3	3	0	0
North & Central America	103	99	81	61	47	39
South America	11	11	10	5	0	0
Total number of DOS	612	594	540	461	388	319

Source: Prada Group annual reports 2011–2015.

allocated to 372 Prada stores, followed by Miu Miu (174 stores), Church's (54 stores), and Car Shoe (five stores) in addition to 27 Prada and 10 Miu Miu franchise stores (Prada, 2015).

In order to ensure the quality of the final products, the procurement and supply network as well as the domestic production facilities of the group tend to be either company-owned or based on a long-term (and often exclusive) collaboration. Prada combines innovative technologies with craftsmanship traditions of production of its goods, often relying on the most unique made-for-Prada materials. Out of 13 company-owned production facilities, 11 are located in Italy (Arezzo, Civitanova Marche, Dolo, Fucecchio, Incisa, Levane, Montegranaro, Montone, Piancastagnaio, Scandicci, Torgiano), 1 in Great Britain (Northampton), and 1 in France (Tannerie Mégisserie Hervy), most recently acquired in October 2014. The production sites are coordinated from Terranuova Bracciolini industrial headquarters in Arezzo, Tuscany, Italy (Prada, 2015). At the same time, following an overall production delocalization trends, a large share of Prada's finished products are produced in global locations in China, Turkey, Vietnam, and Romania for cost-reducing reasons (Passariello, 2011; Tokatli, 2014). The resulting mix of global and domestic production and sourcing in the global marketplace, the quality of Prada is no longer linked exclusively to Made in Italy, but to the quality of the brand that replaces country of origin associations (Cedrola & Battaglia, 2013; Cedrola, Battaglia & Quaranta, 2015; Holt, Quelch & Taylor, 2004).

The group's turnover reached €3,551.7 million in 2014, with 85 % of the total sales coming from the directly controlled retail channel. Despite a slowdown in sales and revenue growth due to a difficult macroeconomic environment, rising global competition, general economic slowdown and some specific market challenges (especially the consequences of an "anti-extravagance campaign" in China[1]), the group preserves its leadership position. Overall, in the period between 2010 and 2014, the company has almost doubled its size as shown on Table 5.2. More specifically, 2014 has shown a 75 % increase in total sales compared to 2010, with a significant consolidation of own retail sales channel, which used to account for a third of company's sales in 2010. European and Northern American markets remain important for the company, but they have demonstrated only moderate growth in terms of sales figures, while Far East (and especially greater China) has nearly doubled since 2010, accounting for €1.1 billion (769 million for greater China) in 2014. Brands other than Prada produce less than stellar growth results, suggesting their role in brand portfolio is not limited entirely to profit-seeking purposes.

COMPANY HISTORY

The history of Prada Group can be divided into four phases: boutique of exclusive baggage and accessories in Milan, Italy (1913–1977); marriage of brand creativity with international expansion strategy (1977–1990s); enhancing brand through anti-commercial projects (2000s–2010s); and consolidating leadership position in business, fashion, and arts patronage (2010s–today). The four phases and milestones in the development of Prada are shown on Fig. 5.1.

Single Focus: Boutique of Exclusive Baggage and Accessories in Milan, Italy (1913–1977)

Prada was founded in 1913 as "Fratelli Prada" (an Italian for "Prada Brothers") by Mario and Martino Prada and was originally conceived as a supplier of exclusive baggage and leather items to the upscale clientele. Mario was the first designer and manager of the company. In its early days, Prada had a single-minded focus to satisfy the need of nobility consumers in high-quality accessories for travels (Moore & Doyle, 2010). It probably resulted from Mario Prada's own experience and passion for travelling

Table 5.2 The Prada Group sales and revenue, 2010–2014 (€ millions)

	2014		2013		2012		2011		2010	
Total Sales	3,513.4		3,548.2		3,256.4		2,523.3		2,017.1	
Wholesale	532.5	15 %	551.6	16 %	592.2	18 %	558.8	22 %	589.7	29 %
Retail	2,980.9	85 %	2,996.6	84 %	2,664.2	82 %	1,964.5	78 %	1,427.4	71 %
Sales by geography*										
Europe	999.6	34 %	1,012	34 %	528.3	16 %	985.7	39 %	843.8	42 %
Americas	391.2	13 %	363.3	12 %	739.6	23 %	392.7	16 %	326.8	16 %
Far East	1,130.2	38 %	1,195.7	40 %	1,160.2	36 %	873	16 %	613.8	30 %
incl. Greater China	769.7	26 %	823.2	27 %	735.6	23 %	544.8	35 %	375.4	19 %
Japan	364.8	12 %	338.7	11 %	293.2	9 %	256.7	22 %	220.9	11 %
Middle East	92.9	3 %	84.5	3 %	NA	NA	NA	NA	NA	NA
Others	2.2	0.1 %	2.5	0 %	51	2 %	15.2	1 %	11.8	1 %

Sales by brand*										
Prada	2,463.2	83 %	2,505.5	84 %	2,649.5	81 %	1,999.3	79 %	1,586.8	79 %
Miu Miu	455.0	15 %	437.5	15 %	512.8	16 %	441.1	17 %	353	18 %
Church's	49.0	2 %	42.7	1 %	68.4	2 %	59.2	2 %	53	3 %
Car Shoe	8.4	0 %	7.5	0 %	19.7	1 %	17	1 %	17.9	1 %
Other	5.3	0 %	3.4	0 %	6	0 %	6.7	0 %	6.2	0 %
Sales by product*										
Leather goods	1,965.6	66 %	2,090.5	70 %	1,678.4	63 %	1,426.5	57 %	1,013.9	50 %
Footwear	448.7	15 %	376.7	13 %	506.2	19 %	560.1	22 %	503.1	25 %
Ready to wear	512.3	17 %	490.6	16 %	452.9	17 %	512.6	20 %	483.6	24 %
Other	54.3	2 %	38.8	1 %	26.6	1 %	24.1	1 %	16.5	1 %
Royalties	38.3		39.1		40.8		32.3		29.6	
Net revenue	3,551.7		3,587.3		3,297.2		2,555.6		2,046.7	
Gross profit	2,550.6		2,648.6		2,376.5		1,828		1,387.9	
Net income	451.0		627.8		625.7		431.9		250.8	
EBITDA	954.3		1,143.2		1,052.5		759.3		535.9	

Note: *2014 and 2013 sales data by geography, brand, and product percentages are based on total of retail sales, 2010–2012 – on total of all sales.
Source: Prada Group annual reports 2011–2015. Retrieved February 11, 2016 from http://www.pradagroup.com/en/investors/financial-reports

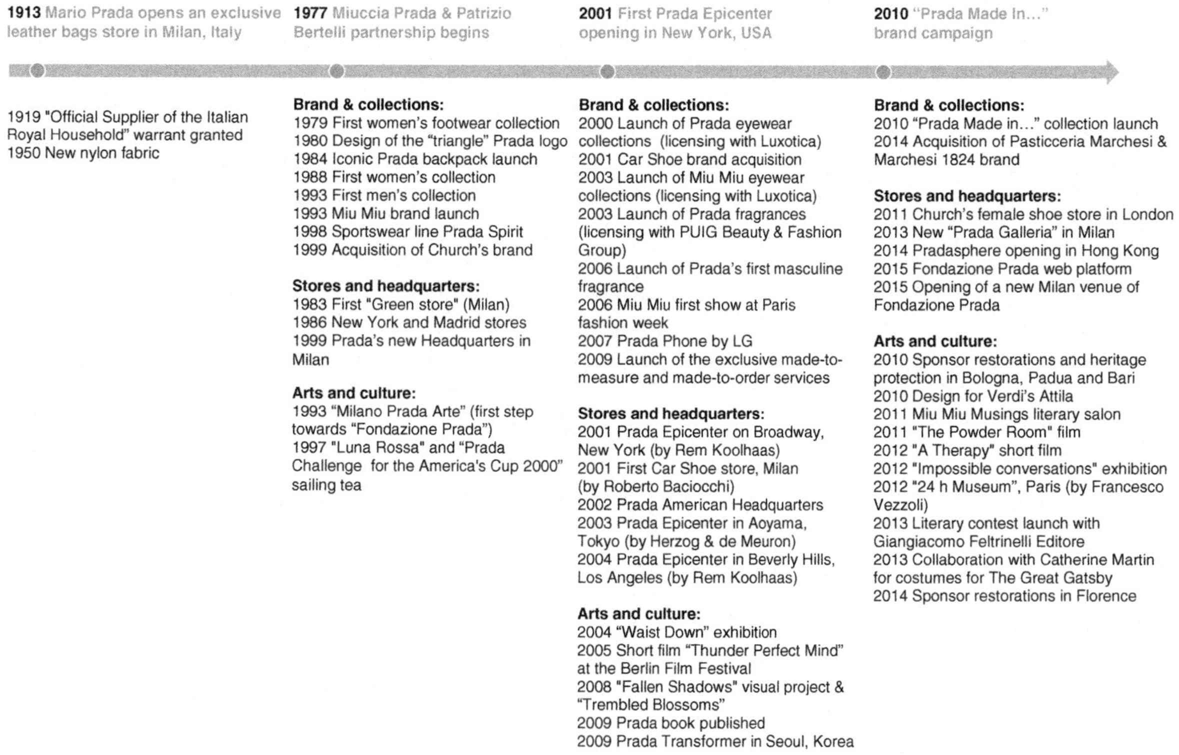

1913 Mario Prada opens an exclusive leather bags store in Milan, Italy

1919 "Official Supplier of the Italian Royal Household" warrant granted
1950 New nylon fabric

1977 Miuccia Prada & Patrizio Bertelli partnership begins

Brand & collections:
1979 First women's footwear collection
1980 Design of the "triangle" Prada logo
1984 Iconic Prada backpack launch
1988 First women's collection
1993 First men's collection
1993 Miu Miu brand launch
1998 Sportswear line Prada Spirit
1999 Acquisition of Church's brand

Stores and headquarters:
1983 First "Green store" (Milan)
1986 New York and Madrid stores
1999 Prada's new Headquarters in Milan

Arts and culture:
1993 "Milano Prada Arte" (first step towards "Fondazione Prada")
1997 "Luna Rossa" and "Prada Challenge for the America's Cup 2000" sailing tea

2001 First Prada Epicenter opening in New York, USA

Brand & collections:
2000 Launch of Prada eyewear collections (licensing with Luxotica)
2001 Car Shoe brand acquisition
2003 Launch of Miu Miu eyewear collections (licensing with Luxotica)
2003 Launch of Prada fragrances (licensing with PUIG Beauty & Fashion Group)
2006 Launch of Prada's first masculine fragrance
2006 Miu Miu first show at Paris fashion week
2007 Prada Phone by LG
2009 Launch of the exclusive made-to-measure and made-to-order services

Stores and headquarters:
2001 Prada Epicenter on Broadway, New York (by Rem Koolhaas)
2001 First Car Shoe store, Milan (by Roberto Baciocchi)
2002 Prada American Headquarters
2003 Prada Epicenter in Aoyama, Tokyo (by Herzog & de Meuron)
2004 Prada Epicenter in Beverly Hills, Los Angeles (by Rem Koolhaas)

Arts and culture:
2004 "Waist Down" exhibition
2005 Short film "Thunder Perfect Mind" at the Berlin Film Festival
2008 "Fallen Shadows" visual project & "Trembled Blossoms"
2009 Prada book published
2009 Prada Transformer in Seoul, Korea

2010 "Prada Made In..." brand campaign

Brand & collections:
2010 "Prada Made in...." collection launch
2014 Acquisition of Pasticceria Marchesi & Marchesi 1824 brand

Stores and headquarters:
2011 Church's female shoe store in London
2013 New "Prada Galleria" in Milan
2014 Pradasphere opening in Hong Kong
2015 Fondazione Prada web platform
2015 Opening of a new Milan venue of Fondazione Prada

Arts and culture:
2010 Sponsor restorations and heritage protection in Bologna, Padua and Bari
2010 Design for Verdi's Attila
2011 Miu Miu Musings literary salon
2011 "The Powder Room" film
2012 "A Therapy" short film
2012 "Impossible conversations" exhibition
2012 "24 h Museum", Paris (by Francesco Vezzoli)
2013 Literary contest launch with Giangiacomo Feltrinelli Editore
2013 Collaboration with Catherine Martin for costumes for The Great Gatsby
2014 Sponsor restorations in Florence

Fig. 5.1   The history of Prada Group since its inception

("Love and fashion affairs," 1996) and changing trends in means of transportation in the twentieth century (Grosvenor, 2015). A strategic location in prestigious Galleria Vittorio Emanuele II in the heart of Milan helped establish brand awareness and secure loyalty of Italian and European aristocrats, which resulted in Prada obtaining the warrant of "Official Supplier of the Italian Royal Household" in 1919. Since then Prada has been officially granted the right to display the royal Savoy coat of arms and figure-of-eight knots surrounding the company logo—a historical "badge of honor" that constitutes brand's heritage.

After Mario's death in 1952, Prada shop passed to the next generation of the Prada family, which is typical of many Italian businesses (Corbetta, 1995). However, quite untypically, it was Mario's daughter, Luisa Prada, to take over since his son expressed no interest in running the store. At that time Prada, unlike for example Gucci, did not have a glaring brand identity and was not well known outside Italy (Moore & Doyle, 2010).

Luisa's daughter, Miuccia Prada (born as Maria Bianchi) had no apparent interest in taking over the family business. Instead, she dedicated her young adulthood to leftist political movements, five years training as a mime artist, being a fierce feminist, and getting a PhD in political science (Felsted, 2015). However, in the end of 1970s, she made a choice to join the family business. Her vision and creativity have eventually created Prada that is known today.

Expanding Brand Geography: Marriage of Brand Creativity with International Expansion Strategy (1977–1990s)

When Miuccia Prada joined the family business, the brand's situation was challenging: distribution was limited and highly localized, design appeared generic and unrecognizable, and the financial situation was not simple. In 1977, Miuccia Prada met Patrizio Bertelli, an owner of a leather business in Tuscany, Italy, and they signed for a partnership that would soon turn Prada into one of the most influential brands in the world. A decade later their partnership in business turned into a marriage.

During the first decade of their collaboration, the company had to undergo two strategic phases: first, search for a differentiation, and second, establish a growth platform (Moore & Doyle, 2010). As a matter of fact, these two phases were largely overlapping and implemented simultaneously. The strategy for company distinction was found partially thanks to Miuccia's non-business background (Prada, 2015). As opposed to other luxury brands present in the market at the time, Prada opted for a simplicity and utilitarianism in its product design, logo, and communication. In 1984, a clean-line black nylon backpack was first launched and soon became a fashion icon, winning over an influential segment of connoisseur customers. Consequently, the same stylistic principle of simplicity and sophisticated sobriety guided Prada in its further growth.

Under the creative direction of Miuccia Prada and production at Patrizio Bertelli's leather factory, Prada launched its first women's footwear collection in 1979, first women's ready-to-wear clothing collection in 1988, and the first menswear, footwear, and accessories in 1993. Moreover, in 1993 Miuccia Prada ideated and launched Miu Miu brand— a youthful and avant-garde extension of her artistic vision. On a more commercial level, the company focused on the factors enabling the future growth under Patrizio Bertelli's lead: (a) wholesale agreements[2] in Europe and the United States with the most strategic multi-brand retail spaces and department stores, such as Saks Inc, Macy's, Neiman Marcus, Barneys, and (b) own retail network growth in Italy and abroad.

In 1983, Prada brand introduced the "Green Store"—a boutique concept characterized by clean and sleek design and particular pale green color scheme, envisioned to contrast the older-fashioned original Prada store in Milan (Prada Group, 2016). The very first "Green Store" opened in Milan in Via della Spiga, but soon it was possible to find these particular "Green Stores," large or small, in New York and Madrid, Paris and London, etc. For Prada, the store became a powerful marketing communication channel and a space to convey brand values and personality viscerally (Irving, 2003). Moreover, directly operated stores, as opposed to other indirect forms, allow much faster and coordinated launches of new collections, monitoring of customers' feedback, and building a direct relationship with customers (Prada, 2015).

It is widely believed that it was the marriage (pun very much intended) of creativity with international business grasp that helped Prada gain its position in the fashion industry. By the end of 1990s, Prada Group became an international business with diversified brand line, wide retail geography, high brand awareness, and reputation of a trendsetter.

Epicenters: Enhancing Brand Through Anti-Commercial Projects (2000s–2010s)

From the end of 1990s to beginning of 2000s, Prada Group has attempted several unsuccessful high-profile acquisitions, including shares of Gucci and Fendi (later sold to LVMH), Helmut Lang (later sold to Japanese Link Theory Holdings), Jil Sander (later sold to British equity firm Change Capital Partners) in its quest to establish its leading position in business (Moore & Doyle, 2010). Two of the more successful acquisitions were Church's (English footwear for men) in 1999 and Car Shoe (upmarket Italian footwear) in 2001— both of them are important assets of the Prada Group up until today. However, the group soon found an alternative non-commercial route to raise awareness and secure leadership, once again rethinking its flagship brand so that it contrasts the rest of the world of luxury. After reviewing trends in global retail, Prada Group has reached a conclusion that their "Prada Green Stores" concept was not allowing for a meaningful differentiation of the brand. So the company sensed the opportunity to complement its typical store format with an atypical and unique super-sized shopping space: The Prada Epicenters. They would help Prada reclaim its position of a creative leader in luxury industry. As Miuccia Prada puts it herself in an interview with The Financial Times in 2003:

> Becoming more famous as a brand means your customer changes. The thing is not to lose the customer and that's why we're undergoing this revolution in our shops. You have to go back, to remember what it means to be sophisticated and to keep growing [...] I like to have beautiful places in which to sell my things. I want to do my work well from every point of view. It's a very simple concept. (Irving, 2003, June 21)

Prada opens the very first Epicenter store on Broadway, New York, United States, an architectural experiment designed by acclaimed architect Rem Koolhaas in 2001. Soon after the first Epicenter, Tokyo Epicenter (by architects Jacques Herzog and Pierre de Meuron) in 2003 and Los Angeles (by Rem Koolhaas) were opened in 2004—all being phenomenal additions or even transformations of urban landscape.

The concept of Epicenters is radically different, because it merges technology, architecture, and design into an experiential space not only for shopping, but also for a range of other services, interactive experiences, and cultural events, transcending pure commerce (Visconti & Di Giuli, 2014). Prada's approach to flagship stores design was soon copied by most of other leading fashion brands. Thanks to the Epicenters, Prada once again set itself against the luxury mainstream, marrying commercial retail with creative architecture, physical space with "immersionary experience" (Schmitt, Rogers & Vrotsos, 2003), world of luxury with the world of arts.

Despite an immeasurable success for the brand reputation, the Epicenters were a costly endeavor. The business shrewdness of Prada once again supplemented its artistic creativity by following some of the more mainstream marketing strategies, for instance, of product democratization (Moore & Doyle, 2010), even though it was a challenge for Miuccia Prada who always valued quality and exclusivity of the brand above all and tried to avoid mass marketing at all costs:

> I'm always checking my stores to see if I like what I see. When selling is too easy I'm always worried. I think that there must be something wrong. It's very dangerous. When we had a belt that sold too much, we pulled it back, just as we did with the Chanel-type bag we did which was a bit of a joke but then it became known as the Prada bag. There were too many copies being made on the street. So we stopped it. (Irving, 2003, June 21)

Nevertheless, in 2000 and 2003 the company signed its eyewear licensing agreement with Italian giant in eyewear Luxottica for its Prada and Miu Miu brands. In 2003, a first Prada fragrance (Prada Exclusive Scents) was launched in partnership with the Spanish PUIG Beauty & Fashion Group, followed by the first masculine fragrance (Prada Amber Man) in 2006 and a number of other scents (Prada Amber Woman in 2004, Infusion d'Iris in 2007, Infusion d'Homme in 2008, Prada Candy in 2011, Prada Luna Rossa in 2012, *Les Infusions de Prada* and Olfactories in 2015). In 2007, LG and Prada together developed an exclusive touchscreen LG Prada smartphone. In 2008 and 2011, subsequent versions entered the market, being quite competitively priced against other smartphones.

It was a challenge for Prada to reconcile the mainstream marketing laws with its "anti-brand/anti-fashion/anti-commercial position" (Tokatli, 2014), however combination of a more democratic product offerings with very visible ground-breaking Epicenter retail space innovations helped the company improve its financial bottom-line, without diluting the brand creative luxury reputation.

Placeless Brand: Consolidating Leadership Position in Business, Fashion, and Arts Patronage (2010s–Today)

Prada Group has entered the decade of 2010s as a global leader in luxury business and consequently the company strategy has been revolving around consolidating such leadership position. It continues to use art, architecture, cinema and culture projects to express the brand's core values of creativity, counter-stream sense of style, and special, temporal, and disciplinary connectivity (Visconti & Di Giuli, 2014). In 2010, Prada launched a "Prada Made in ..." limited collection that featured manufacturing excellence from all over the world: traditional embroidered dresses from India, exclusive jeans from Japan, alpaca sweaters from Peru, and tartan kilts from Scotland. Each product label featured the origin of production, for instance "Prada Milano, Made in Scotland." The brand communication surrounding the collection emphasized how global physical and intellectual interconnectedness, including Prada's authenticity and creativity, transcends places of production (Tokatli, 2014; Visconti & Di Giuli, 2014). Miuccia Prada reportedly introduced this collection by saying, "Made in Italy? Who cares!" (Bumpus, 2010).

Shortly after "Prada Made in ...," the company made another global statement. On June 24, 2011, Prada Group listed 20 % of its shares on the Hong Kong stock exchange, where the company was valued at €9.2 billion (Prada Group, 2016). In 2014, Prada acquired a major share of historic pastry shop Marchesi 1824 in Milan and reopened its famous pastry shop (Pasticceria Marchesi), adding a signature pale green color to the interior design. Despite global orientation, Prada preserves its connection to the Milan "magic circle"[3] (Dunford, 2006) and the acquisition and reopening of the meaningful historic pastry shop allowed the brand to protect its cultural "brand myth" (Holt, 2004) of connection to distinct Milanese culture of doing both business and fashion.

In the same period, Prada Group has also strengthened the role of Fondazione Prada; originally, a foundation for contemporary art exhibitions established in 1993, and in 2010s—a comprehensive think tank and operative center for the Group's corporate social responsibility

(CSR) and cultural activities. Fondazione Prada has been since involved in a range of activities including architecture, philosophy, science, design, reality television, and cinema (Fondazione Prada, 2016). Numerous films (including short and animated films and commercials) were made thanks to collaboration of Fondazione Prada with the world of cinema. In 2010, Miuccia Prada debuted as an arts director for a Verdi's Attila opera staged at the Metropolitan Museum of New York, United States. In 2013, she collaborated with the famous costume designer Catherine Martin for "The Great Gatsby" movie (Binkley, 2013). Additionally, the Prada Group sponsored various restorations and cultural heritage programs in the Italian cities of Bologna, Padua, Bari, and Florence.

Besides continuous growth of the new retail locations around the world (in 2015 there were 605 stores in 70 countries, 18 new opening compared to year ago, almost double, compared to 2010), Prada today invests into corporate locations and auto-celebrative venues. In 2013, a new "Prada Galleria" was opened in front of its historical location in Milan. In 2014, in collaboration with Rem Koolhaas, Prada built a Prada Transformer, a temporary exhibition space in Seoul, Korea, that incorporated different surfaces that rotated to become a stage for a movie presentation, a contemporary art exhibition, a cultural event, or a fashion display (Visconti & Di Giuli, 2014). In 2014, a Pradasphere, an exhibition exploring the universe of Prada, was opened in Hong Kong. In 2015, a new Milan venue of Fondazione Prada was opened. All in all, the Prada Group continues to strengthen its leadership position as a creative, ambitious, and trendsetting global business, yet deeply grounded in Milan culture of luxury. The following section is devoted to a detailed presentation of the five brands that make up the Prada Group's portfolio.

BRAND PORTFOLIO STRATEGY

The strength of a brand is inextricably linked to the business model that supports it,[4] being the only way a firm can ensure the effective fulfillment of the needs expressed by the consumer at the time of purchase (Kapferer, 2008). Effectiveness and efficiency of the Prada Group's business model were guaranteed by the careful choices by the CEO Patrizio Bertelli, who made a number of innovations in group's business processes—from production to distribution—and who has been able to give up the acquisition of brands such as Gucci and Helmut Lang in which Prada Group had decided to get involved in the early 1990s. The current business policy of Prada Group is firmly focused on core brands, mostly Prada and Miu Miu, with special interest in expanding to emerging markets, most notably Russia, China, and Africa (Bertelli, 2012).

The most important choice supported by Patrizio Bertelli has been to remain independent, in a period where the luxury industry is consolidating through continuous mergers and acquisitions (Lipovetsky & Roux, 2003; Kapferer & Bastien, 2009; Kapferer, 2012). Such independence is fundamental for the ability to control all of the activities undertaken by the brand, from the management of raw materials and the quality control of workmanship, to the speed with which the collections are made available to consumers through the brand distribution network in the world (Bertelli, 2012). The choice not to be incorporated into large luxury conglomerates, and the consequent choice to focus on the development of a few selected brands, can be traced back to the stability of Prada corporate culture, as stated by Patrizio Bertelli, "Although we have often had to change our plans, the way we manage the company has remained constant" (Bertelli, 2012, p. 39). It is exactly this ability to remain faithful to itself while maintaining an open outlook that allowed the Prada brand to anticipate the spirit of its time and influence on global luxury fashion tastes.

The elitism perception of Prada and Miu Miu brands is ensured by the sophisticated design, related to the artistic direction by Miuccia Prada, as well as the creation of a myth about her as an artist. The unconventional background of Miuccia Prada has contributed to enhance the myth around designer's life story and creativity, making her one of the icons in the artistic environment (Dion & Arnould, 2011). The quest for a sophisticated design can also be seen in the selection of acquired brands that are now part of the group. The next section will briefly describe the main features of each brand.

Prada

The Prada brand, worn by "the Devil"[5] and millions of customers worldwide, is doubtlessly one of the global symbols of luxury. Despite its unconventional "anti-fashion" and "anti-luxury" design appeal, Prada is the only Italian-owned brand ranked in Interbrand luxury list (Interbrand, 2015). The main efforts of Prada Group are devoted to the development and increase of the Prada brand value, accounting for 81.2 % of total sale revenues of the group, corresponding to €1.46 billion (from January to July 2015). Prada's avant-garde creativity is expressed through the merchandise from leather goods to ready to wear clothing, supported by group's art-related strategies and technological innovation, as well as embodied in retail locations, reaching its maximum expression in the concept of Prada Epicenters, which will be discussed in more detail later in this chapter.

Miu Miu

Embracing both "*couture savoir-faire* and refined experimentalism," Miu Miu brand, created as a space for Miuccia Prada's provocative creativity in 1993, is dichotomous to sober and minimalism style of the flagship brand Prada. Miu Miu is the second most important group's brand with net sales of €293.92 million at the end of July 2015, corresponding to 16.3 % of total revenues.

It's quite common for fashion luxury brands to create a secondary, less-expensive line to expand their business and ensure that even less wealthy customers can buy into the brand experience; think of Emporio Armani, D&G, Just Cavalli, etc. Despite apparent similarities, Miu Miu does not entirely fit into a typical secondary brand strategy. On one hand, Miu Miu targets younger clientele and tends to use more affordable materials, on the other—the prices are not necessarily lower than that of Prada, rather they are "in line with the quality of the product," according to an interview with Bertelli (Kaiser, 2006). Miu Miu's strategy therefore is not about being Prada's "younger sister," but a "friendly competitor" with a unique standout identity (Passariello, 2010).

Church's

Church's is a historical English brand of men's shoes founded in 1873 in Northampton with a know-how based on family experience of shoe-making dating back to 1675. The handicraft brand was acquired by Prada Group in 1999 and today it corresponds to 2.1 % of total revenues or €38.38 million of net sales. The brand strategy is guided by targeting a customer base looking for high-quality craftsmanship shows with a classic elegant design. Recently, the brand has introduced for the very first time a women's line stylistically aligned to the offer in the men's segment.

Car Shoe

Car Shoe was founded in Italy in 1963 by Gianni Mostile and acquired by Prada Group in 2001. The Car Shoe moccasins are originally designed using high quality materials and handmade crafstmanship to enhance the experience of driving sports cars. The brand's target is elegant clientele with the needs of classic shoes for leisure time. With net sales of €5.52 million (as of end of July 2015), the brand corresponds to 0.3 % of total revenues of Prada Group.

Marchesi 1824

In March 2014, Prada acquired 80 % of Marchesi—the pastry shop opened by Angelo Marchesi in 1824 inside an elegant eighteenth century building—with the intention of developing this high-level family operated Milanese brand (Pasticceria Marchesi, 2016). The aim of Prada Group is to transform this café into an "institution" in the city of Milan, both for locals and for tourists (Marchesi, 2016) by enhancing its communication, strengthening the contact with the consumer, and increasing the number of mono-brand shops in other emblematic locations. In September 2015, the second shop opened in another exclusive location in the "Milan magic circle" in Via Monte Napoleone, preserving the brand's long-standing tradition of excellence.

CREATIVE BRAND BUILDING AT THE INTERSECTION OF ART, TECHNOLOGY, AND CONSUMER EXPERIENCE

With a globally renowned "fashionless fashion" reputation, Prada's brand building strategy reflects on how strategic, but somehow unconventional choices can help establish distinctive place in such a competitive industry as fashion. In addition to design and creative brand vision discussed previously, among the main tools that allowed Prada to find and occupy a peculiar place in the heads and wardrobes of influential connoisseur customers are: a close link between arts and the brand, strategic use of technology to establish consumer-brand connection, and investment into innovative and audacious architectural projects such as Prada Epicenters.

Artful Brand Building

One of the most powerful strategies embodied by the Prada brand is uniting the worlds of fashion and contemporary art. Today main luxury players, such as Chanel or Hermès, use the bond with the art in a strategic way (Weidemann & Hennings, 2013), but not all of the aspiring fashion companies are able to reach a great response from the artistic world. Contrarily, the Prada brand is very versed into the world of culture and art, thanks to Miuccia Prada and Patrizio Bertelli's genuine interest and active participation in the global visual art scene. According to Massimiliano Gioni, curator of the Trussardi Foundation and director of the New Museum in New York City as well as of the art section of the Venice Biennale, Prada can be considered one of the most active companies in the field of art. Moreover, the Italian contemporary art market would not be the same without the support of these new patrons from the fashion luxury business world (Pappalardo, 2014). For example, some internationally renowned artists like Francesco Vezzoli[6] would probably not enjoy the same international recognition without the support of the Prada Foundation, acted as a real institution for the support of the art. The Prada Foundation chaired by Miuccia Prada and Patrizio Bertelli was inaugurated in 1993 and has more than twenty years of experience in promotion of contemporary art. Since May 2015, the Foundation has opened a new exhibition area in Milan, in a building restored by architect Rem Koolhaas (Fondazione Prada, 2016; Ryan, 2007). The partnership with leading international architects constitutes another strength for the brand, which allowed Prada to increase the visibility of its retail outlets in the world, to create a constantly evolving brand experience space, and first-handedly narrate its brand essence to the customers (Pine & Gilmore, 1999; Vescovi & Checchinato, 2004).

Technology-Enhanced Brand Experience

Another source of innovation for Prada in addition to the relationship with the contemporary art world is investments in technology. Among the most innovative projects may include the wearable computer, the shoe phone, or the Prada laptop: all projects remained so far in a conceptual condition only (Prada, 2009). A technological project that has instead turned into reality is the Prada smartphone realized in 2007 through collaboration with LG, with which Prada has greatly contributed to the evolution of touchscreen mobile devices. The LG Prada touchscreen technology was among the first to enter the market—the same year as the iPhone. The smartphone stylishly combined functionality with avant-garde design, and reissued two successor versions in 2008 and 2011. While the very first LG Prada smartphone was sold at a price premium compared to other touchscreen devices (e.g., iPhone), the successors were priced very competitively against the rest of Android smartphones (e.g., HTC Sensation or Sony Ericsson Xperia), showing that Prada-LG collaboration started off as a "luxury-fication" of technology, but consequently moved into competing against other smartphones based on their functionality. Reducing Prada's brand image to just a design element has not proved very successful in the longer run in such innovation-driven market as touchscreen smartphones.

Possibly the most interesting projects Prada involved with technology are related to retail experiences, with projects especially created to be included in the Epicenters. Most of the Prada technological innovations were made and designed by the architectural studio Oma, which also followed the realization of some of the conceptual retail spaces (Oma, 2016). One of the activities that was applied relates to Radio-frequency identification (RFID), or the electronic tags used for an evolved Customer Relationship Management (CRM). These cards were created to replace the bar codes inserted into every Prada labels permanently (Prada, 2009). RFID are intended to be an interface between the brand and the customer who can use them to search more information about the product by interacting directly with the staff or from home via Prada website. This technology is directly related to Prada Customer Cards for loyal customers. Through such devices the customer is immediately recognizable by the sales staff, which can thus ensure a highly customized shopping experience, by proposing the right size or the preferred colors for every single customer (Prada, 2009). At the same time the relationship is interactive as the same customer can use his/her card to create a personal virtual closet accessible online or ask for more information about a product (RFID Journal, 2002).

Other technological innovations introduced within the Epicenters are the dressing rooms, the Kiosks, and the Peep Shows. The first are innovative dressing rooms in which the customer is once again active part of the shopping experience being able to consult the inventory, control the dressing area's lighting, place orders and ask questions about the products, or even adjust the transparency of the same dressing room walls (Prada, 2009). Kiosks and Peep Shows are instead interactive spaces inside the Epicentres where the customer can directly seek the Prada website or even choose between a number of different kinds of channels as special video productions, backstage of fashion shows, videos of the store's security cameras, TV channel, home videos, and old movies (Prada, 2009).

Immersionary Brand Experiences: Prada Green Stores and Epicenters

Retail spaces of fashion brands do not only sell products, they are spaces that spread the aura of the designer by ensuring a "marketing of adoration" and creating a dialogue with consumers in the space entirely dedicated to them (Dion & Arnould, 2011).

Prada's first original retail concept, Green Stores designed by the architect Roberto Baciocchi, opened in Milan in 1983. It was characterized by a particular shade of light green that has been soon recognized as "green Prada." From that moment on, Prada opened a network of Green Stores all over the world (Prada, 2009). The choice to focus on the dissemination of retail spaces primarily reflects the need to have a direct contact with the end consumer, which ensures a better control of brand image.

Such strategy, however, may involve problems for luxury companies as the increase of directly operated stores ensures the growth of brand awareness but, at the same time, undermines the perception of rarity and elitism that luxury brands must be able to preserve in the eyes of the consumers (De Barnier, Falcy & Valette-Florence, 2012; Kapferer, 2012). Prada gracefully glossed the danger of an excessive spread of its Green Stores all over the world by introducing, in addition to Green Stores, of a conceptually different retail space—the Epicenters.

There are three "official" Prada Epicenters, in New York, Los Angeles and Tokyo (Prada, 2009, 2016), but new boutique opened in 2013 in Galleria

Vittorio Emanuele II in Milan and the London store are often referred to as "other" Prada Epicenters (Visconti & Di Giuli, 2014; Oma, 2016). The Epicenters were designed by internationally acclaimed architects such as Rem Koolhaas (New York and Los Angeles), and Herzog & de Meuron (Tokyo), all winners of the Pritzker Prize (the Nobel Prize of architecture) (Fig. 5.2).

Fig. 5.2 Prada Epicenters in Tokyo (left) and New York (bottom right), and new Prada stores at Galleria Vittorio Veneto, Milan (top right) (*Source*: Photo by Claudia Panunzio (Tokyo), Elena Cedrola (Milan), and Inna Litvinova (New York))

The very first Prada Epicenter in New York was a product of three-year research into shopping trends worldwide and was conceived as a unique flagship—dramatically different from common flagship stores of major luxury brands. This Epicenter is definitely the ultimate expression of a mix of technology, art, and architecture wanted by Prada to ensure the consumer a unique experience, as well as the first Epicenter in which most of the innovations described in the previous paragraph have been tested for the first time.

Inside it features a "wood wave that undulates from street level to the floor below, motorized hanging display cages that travel on tracks in the ceiling, and a flip-out stage for special events" (Prada, 2009, p. 432). This multi-functional wave may also host concerts, film screenings, exhibitions, and special events. Another essential element of New York Epicenter is "the wall" that covers the entire length of a block, which it is used as canvas for contemporary graphics that are changed repeatedly to modify the store atmosphere from time to time. New York Epicenter gained success immediately and remains one of the greatest exemplars of flagship stores worldwide (Prada, 2009).

The Tokyo Epicenter in prestigious Aoyama district, recognized as one of the 10th Tokyo's best works of architecture (Rawlings, 2012), followed shortly after New York. The six-floor structure was designed to form a continuum with the surrounding space. The building is transparent and the city is constantly reflected in the glass surface with which the entire building is built. The construction of the building has also enabled the creation of the Prada Plaza—a public space at the heart of the city. The interior is characterized by elements of design and technology, such as the "snorkels," special interfaces that transmit sounds, lights, and images (Prada, 2009, 2016).

After the success of the New York and Tokyo spaces, follow the openings of the Los Angeles Prada Epicenter located on the historic Rodeo Drive in Beverly Hills. The design is the inverse of New York as "a wave starts at street level and rises to the second floor before dropping back down again" (Prada, 2016). This building does not have a door but is widely opened to the street. The internal spaces are characterized by a resin sponge that has been specially fabricated for this retail space, while the main stairs is formed from a special material that creates the curious effect of reducing or enlarging the size of the store depending on the number of actual clients. Also, this space—as the New York Epicenter—is defined by wallpaper, which easily allows the renewal of the internal atmosphere (Prada, 2009).

The design and management of Prada Epicenters is dramatically different as their ultimate goal is to create a genuine experimental laboratory for the brand (Prada, 2009). Entertainment spaces are able to sell not only products or services but, first of all, a corporate brand image (Schmitt & Simonson, 1997). In this regard we believe that Prada Epicenters are fully included in what Kozinets and colleagues (2002) identify as themed flagship brand store, or spaces able to generate revenues from entertainment activities dedicated to brand building, instead of products and services (Kozinets et al., 2002).

DISCUSSION AND IMPLICATION

One of a few luxury groups that are still independent, Prada has built its success thanks to high-level production standards, design-oriented and innovative, as well as effective and efficient business model oriented toward the direct contact with consumers. The brand value is built and strengthened thanks to a high share of retail locations managed directly by the group, both nationally and internationally. On the other hand, counter-mainstream innovation is guaranteed by the creative leadership by Miuccia Prada, the "myth" around her life story, and an ever-growing intimate contact of the group with the world of the visual art, in particular with that of contemporary architecture and avant-garde.

The Prada brand is not only an internationally acclaimed symbol of "fashionless fashion," but also a case where the strategic orientation toward independence complements creative vision of uniqueness in building the brand, as we know it today.

Throughout its history, Prada—both as a brand and as a group—relied on some of the most unusual strategies for luxury brands: from using such plain material as nylon to create a fashion icon backpack in 1984, abstaining from mergers with multinational luxury giants, inventing the concept of Epicenters and other multi-functional cultural and retail spaces, challenging own strength of "Made in Italy" with provocative "Made in Worlds" campaign, to extensively collaborating with the world of arts. At the same time, besides a constant search for distinction, Prada brand has been built up on an appropriate business model that ensures efficiency, functionality, and resistance through time (Kapferer, 2008), such as wide national and international geography of directly managed retail locations, orientation at high quality of production, managerial coherence, etc. Some of the common denominators in realization of such brand strategy have been Prada's ability to connect the world of fashion and design with other realities: visual arts, technology, and contemporary architecture.

Epicenters ultimately represent the quintessence of bringing together various brand building elements in which Prada excels. First, they resulted from a careful examination of contemporary retail trends in order to rework them into the most original retail experience for consumers including leisure activities, art works, aesthetic atmosphere, interactive technological devices etc., which allowed the brand to go against the mainstream once again. As theme brand flagship store, their purpose was envisioned to take the brand concept to an extreme level thanks to the narrative shared with consumers through various activities going beyond mere shopping.

Second, despite being a controversial investment in strictly financial terms, they served a strategic and organizational purpose of extending the network of company's directly operated stores and demonstrating—loud and clear—that the brand's intention is to remain unique and independent. In other words, budgets for flagships brand stores should be viewed rather as part of a long-term brand building strategy.

Third, they merge the world of fashion with visual arts, technology, and contemporary architecture. Besides being architectural avant-garde spaces, Epicenters create a real laboratory for generating new forms of brand interaction with the surrounding physical and cultural landscapes. In this way, the experience of the brand can be open not only to the ultimate consumer, but also to the simple observer, who can enjoy the Prada Epicenter space for a concert or a show. On the other hand, Epicenters also create an exclusive experience for their core customers of influential connoisseurs, thanks to technological innovations such as customer card linked to RFID, smart dressing rooms, kiosks, and peep rooms. Owing to constant interaction with both core consumers and transient observers, the Epicenters help Prada formulate and produce the reflection about contemporary society—the reflection that keeps feeding brand vision and creativity.

Finally, they are embodiment and extension of the idealization of Prada's brand myth, especially the aura of adoration used as a marketing lever (Dion & Arnould 2011) that surrounds the brand with its "anti-fashion" reputation.

Prada Epicenters are not the sole base of Prada's success in brand strategy, but they represent a synergy of the core values the brand believes in and cultivates throughout its brand building (Borghini et al., 2009). The merger of business strategy oriented at independence and direct control over retail, managerial coherence, well-delineated brand portfolio, with quest for aesthetic and cultural distinction, constant search for updated "anti-fashion" image by connecting to the contemporary art scene, well-studied but unconventional use of technology, arts and architecture—all these elements blend together to build a creative, ambitious, and trendsetting global business and brand of Prada.

NOTES

1. In 2013, the Chinese government launched a campaign to fight against corruption and lavish spending of the governmental officials on banquets, vacation, and gifts with the use of public money. This has led to a dramatic decrease in the sales of luxury items, the first negative trend for the luxury sales in decades.
2. In the late 1980s, when Prada bags, shoes, and accessories were in high demand by the customers, the most popular items were sold to retailers only together with relatively little-known women's ready-to-wear items and, later in 1990s, with secondary Miu Miu, men's and sportswear lines (Tokatli, 2014).
3. Just like with Parisian *haute couture* and Florentine leather industries, Milan's "magic circle" stands for an agglomerate of ready-to-wear industry players, who collectively build up the cultural capital in fashion. Such cultural capital is used both as an organizational asset (e.g., knowledge, human resources availability, partnership opportunities, cost containment, innovation) for the companies that come to operate in and around Milan, and as a strategic marketing leverage (e.g., image, reputation, competitive advantage) for the companies projecting their link to Milan while working with the rest of the world.
4. All the data for the brand portfolio section are referred to Interim Financial Report, 2015 from January to July 2015, as the Annual Report of Prada Group was unavailable when this case was written.
5. *The Devil Wears Prada* is a 2006 comedy-drama (among 2006's top 20 both in the United States and abroad) starring Anne Hathaway, Meryl Streep, Emily Blunt, Stanley Tucci, and others. It is a film adaptation of Lauren Weisberger's 2003 book with the same name.
6. Francesco Vezzoli (b. 1971, Brescia, Italy) studied at the Central St. Martin's School of Art in London and currently lives and works in Milan. His work has been exhibited at many institutions.

REFERENCES

Bertelli, P. (2012). Prada's CEO on staying independent in a consolidating industry. *Harvard Business Review*, *90*(9), 39–42.

Betts, K. (2005). Miuccia Prada. *Time*. Retrieved from http://content.time.com/time/specials/packages/article/0,28804,1972656_1972696_1973344,00.html

Binkley, C. (2013, April 18). How Prada created a "Gatsby" fashion moment. *Wall Street Journal.* Retrieved from http://www.wsj.com/articles/ SB10001424127887324 493704578428790345230204

Borghini, S., Diamond, N., Kozinets, R. V., McGrath, M. A., Muniz, A. M., & Sherry, J. F. (2009). Why are themed brand stores so powerful? Retail brand ideology at American Girl Place. *Journal of Retailing, 85*(3), 363–375. doi:10.1016/j.jretai.2009.05.003

Bumpus, J. (2010, September 29). Prada's new label. *Vogue.* Retrieved from http://www.vogue.co.uk/news/2010/09/29/prada-country-of-origin-labels

Cedrola, E., Battaglia, L., & Quaranta, A. G. (2015). The country of origin effect (COO) in the industrial sectors: The results of an empirical study. *In Proceedings of the 14th International Congress Marketing Trends.* Paris, France.

Cedrola, E., & Battaglia, L. (2013). Country-of-origin effect and firm reputation influence in business-to-business markets with high cultural distance. *Journal of Global Scholars of Marketing Science, 23*(4), 394–408. doi:10.1080/ 21639159.2013.818280

Corbetta, G. (1995). Patterns of development of family businesses in Italy. *Family Business Review, 8*(4), 255–265. doi:10.1111/j.1741-6248.1995.00255.x

De Barnier, V., Falcy, S., & Valette-Florence, P. (2012). Do consumers perceive three levels of luxury? A comparison of accessible, intermediate and inaccessible luxury brands. *Journal of Brand Management, 19*(7), 623–636. doi:10.1057/ bm.2012.11

Dion, D., & Arnould, E. (2011). Retail luxury strategy: assembling charisma through art and magic. *Journal of Retailing, 87*(4), 502–520. doi:10.1016/j. jretai.2011.09.001

Dunford, M. (2006). Industrial districts, magic circles, and the restructuring of the Italian textiles and clothing chain. *Economic Geography, 82*(1), 27–59. doi:10.1111/j.1944-8287.2006.tb00287.x

Felsted, A. (2015). Business pioneers in fashion & retail. *The Financial Times.* Retrieved from http://www.ft.com/cms/s/2/31b2c0f4-cc95-11e4-b5a5-00144feab7de.html#axzz4CuCelDJp

Fondazione Prada. (2016). *Fondazione Prada.* Retrieved from http://www.fon dazioneprada.org/?lang=en

Grosvenor, C. (2015, July 7). From suitcases to Oscar gowns, from Milan to the World. Retrieved from http://www.lifeinitaly.com/fashion/prada.asp

Holt, D. B. (2004). *How brands become icons: the principles of cultural branding.* Boston: Harvard Business Press.

Holt, D. B., Quelch, J. A., & Taylor, E. L. (2004). How global brands compete. *Harvard Business Review, 82*(9), 68–75.

Interbrand. (2015). Best global brands 2015. Retrieved from http://interbrand. com/best-brands/best-global-brands/2015/ranking/

Irving, M. (2003, June 21). Being Miuccia she has created one of the most coveted brands in fashion, but is uneasy with the connotations this world evokes. As Miuccia Prada unveils a new Tokyo store, she talks to Mark Irving about art, commerce and a passion for architecture. *Financial Times.* Retrieved from http://search.proquest.com/docview/249502205? accountid=14604

Kaiser, A. (2006, March 3). Miu Miu comes into its own. *WWD, 191*(46), 7. Retrieved from http://search.proquest.com/docview/231117166?accountid= 12180

Kapferer, J. (2008). *The new strategic brand management: creating and sustaining brand equity long term.* London: Kogan-Page.

Kapferer, J. N. (2012). Abundant rarity: the key to luxury growth. *Business Horizons, 55*(5), 453–462. doi:10.1016/j.bushor.2012.04.002

Kapferer, J.-N., & Bastien, V. (2009). The specificity of luxury management: turning marketing upside down. *Journal of Brand Management, 16*(5–6), 311–322. doi:10.1057/bm.2008.51

Kozinets, R. V., Sherry, J. F., DeBerry-Spence, B., Duhachek, A., Nuttavuthisit, K., & Storm, D. (2002). Themed flagship brand stores in the new millennium: theory, practice, prospects. *Journal of Retailing, 78*(1), 17–29. doi:10.1016/ S0022-4359(01)00063-X

Lipovetsky, G., & Roux, E. (2003). *Le luxe éternel. de l'Age du Sacré au Temps des Marques.* Paris: Gallimard.

Love and fashion affairs: Prada fall/winter1996-97. (1996, September 30). *Business World.* Retrieved from http://search.proquest.com/docview/ 234012401?accountid=12180

Marchesi. (2016). Marchesi 1824. Retrieved from http://www.pradagroup.com/ en/brands/marchesi-1824

Moore, C. M., Doherty, A. M., & Doyle, S. A. (2010). Flagship stores as a market entry method: The perspective of luxury fashion retailing. *European Journal of Marketing, 44*(1/2), 139–161. doi:10.1108/03090561011008646

Moore, C. M., & Doyle, S. A. (2010). The evolution of a luxury brand: the case of Prada. *International Journal of Retail & Distribution Management, 38*(11/ 12), 915–927. doi:10.1108/09590551011085984

Oma. (2016). Oma office work search. Retrieved from http://oma.eu/projects/ prada-epicenter-london

Pappalardo, D. (2014). Gioni: Ecco la mia nuova Biennale. Retrieved from www. repubblica.it/cultura/2014/11/30/news/gioni_ecco_la_mia_nuova_bien nale-101811389

Passariello, C. (2010, October 6). In bloom: Miu Miu comes of age. *Wall Street Journal* Retrieved from http://search.proquest.com/docview/756549320? accountid=12180

Passariello, C. (2011, June 24). Prada is making fashion in China. *Wall Street Journal*. Retrieved from http://www.wsj.com/articles/ SB1000142405270230 423120457640368096786692

Pasticceria Marchesi. (2016). Marchesi 1824. Retrieved from http://www.pastic ceriamarchesi.it/index

Pine, B. J., & Gilmore, J. H. (1999). *The experience economy: work is theatre & every business a stage*. Boston: Harvard Business Press. doi:10.1080/ 02642069700000028

Prada (2009). *Prada*. Milano: Progetto Prada Arte.

Prada. (2015). Company profile-October 2015. Retrieved from http://www. pradagroup.com/uploads/prada/document/document/40/PRADA_ GROUP_Company_Profile_October_2015_ENG.pdf

Prada. (2016). Prada Epicenters. Retrieved from http://www.prada.com/it/a-future-archive/epicenters.html

Prada Group. (2016). Annual reports. Retrieved from http://www.pradagroup. com/en/investors/financial-reports

Rawlings, A. (2012). 10 of Tokyo's best works of architecture. *The Guardian Website*. Retrieved from http://www.theguardian.com/travel/2012/feb/ 01/top-10-buildings-architecture-tokyo

RFID Journal. (2002, June 24). Learning from Prada. Retrieved from http:// www.rfidjournal.com/articles/view?196/

Ryan, N. (2007). Prada and the art of patronage. *Fashion Theory, 11*(1), 7–24. doi:10.2752/136270407779934588

Schmitt, B., Rogers, D., & Vrotsos, K. (2003). *There's no business that's not show business: marketing in an experience culture*. New Jersey: FT Press.

Schmitt, B., & Simonson, A. (1997). *Marketing aesthetics: the strategic management of brands, identity, and image*. New York: The Free Press.

Tokatli, N. (2014). "Made in Italy? Who cares!" Prada's new economic geography. *Geoforum, 54*, 1–9. doi:10.1016/j.geoforum.2014.03.005

Vescovi, T., & Checchinato, F. (2004). Luoghi d'esperienza e strategie competitive nel dettaglio. *Micro & Macro Marketing, 3*, 595–608. doi:10.1431/18864

Visconti, L. M., & Di Giuli, A. (2014). Principles and levels of Mediterranean connectivity: evidence from Prada's "Made in Worlds" brand strategy. *Journal of Consumer Behaviour, 13*(3), 164–175. doi:10.1002/cb.1477

Weidemann, K. P., & Henningss, N. (2013). *Luxury marketing a challenge for theory and practice*. Wiesbaden: Springer Gabler. doi:10.1007/978-3-8349-4399-6

Dr. Stefania Masè is an adjunct professor (ATER - Attaché Temporaire d'Enseignement et de Recherche) at the University of Pau and the Adour Region, France, where she teaches Marketing and International Marketing. She is also a professor of Marketing Metrics at the University of Macerata, Italy. Her current research interests include luxury goods, consumer behaviour, and marketing of culture and the arts.

Ksenia Silchenko currently pursues her PhD in Economics and Management at the University of Macerata, Italy. Her educational background is in Intercultural Studies and before starting her PhD, she worked as a Consumer Insights Researcher and Analyst for a global marketing consultancy firm. Her research interests lie in the field of marketing and consumer behavior, brand management, value (co)creation, and marketing communication.

CHAPTER 6

Louis Vuitton's Art-Based Strategy to Communicate Exclusivity and Prestige

Stefania Masè and Elena Cedrola

Abstract The recent global luxury industry has transformed from a constellation of small and medium-sized enterprises to a few large luxury conglomerates. This new structure, along with growing foreign markets such as Asia, has caused an increase in sales volumes, resulting in production that is more industrial than handcrafted. These changes decrease exclusiveness for luxury brands, which may lead to commoditization of the luxury brands in consumers' eyes.

To alleviate this commoditization, many luxury brands work to communicate exclusivity and prestige through strategic arts sponsorships, philanthropic activities, and limited collections in collaboration with artists. These activities binding luxury brands with the art world constitute an art-based strategy named *artification*. This approach is described via the behavior of luxury brand Louis Vuitton, with a particular focus on the relationship that links the French luxury brand together with the

S. Masè (✉)
Atlantic Pyrenees department, Pau-Bayonne University School of Management, University of Pau and the Adour Region, Pau, Nouvelle Aquitaine, France

E. Cedrola
Department of Economics and Law, University of Macerata, Macerata, Italy

© The Author(s) 2017   155
B. Jin, E. Cedrola (eds.), *Fashion Branding and Communication*,
Palgrave Studies in Practice: Global Fashion Brand Management,
DOI 10.1057/978-1-137-52343-3_6

contemporary Japanese artists Takashi Murakami and Yayoi Kusama. Via a qualitative analysis, we identify how these art-based strategies utilize different contact points with the art world, ranging from sponsorships to advertising to product design, in order to communicate an image of exclusiveness and prestige for luxury brands.

Keywords Luxury brands · Commoditization · Co-branding · Art-based Strategy · *Artification*

INTRODUCTION

Luxury brands are increasingly applying strategies based on their relationship with the art world, known collectively as *artification* strategies (Kapferer, 2012, 2014; Masè, 2016). The term *artification*, as used in sociology of art, describes the process of treating non-art objects as art (Naukkarinen, 2012; Heinich & Shapiro, 2012). In management studies, the same term applies to the efforts that luxury firms take to bind their brands and products to the art world (Kapferer, 2014). These efforts involve luxury brands in multiple art-related activities, including arts sponsorships and philanthropy; funding of museums, auction houses, or art fairs in collaboration with artists for the realization of limited collections; advertising and communications activities (Kapferer, 2012; Masè, 2016). This strategy aims to ensure perceptions of exclusiveness among consumers and stimulation of sales, and for this reason, it has become a fundamental strategy for luxury brands facing commoditization[1] problems. To grow in the industry, luxury brands oftentimes penetrate global markets by increasing their production with low-cost collections, such as ready-to-wear. This creates a problem of commoditization that counters one of the core tenets of luxury, that of rarity and exclusiveness (Dubois, Laurent, & Czellar, 2001; Vigneron & Johnson, 1999, 2004).

Louis Vuitton (LV), the number one luxury brand in the world (Cavender & Kincade, 2014; Interbrand, 2016) was established in 1854 and has since become one of the most famous producers of luxury goods for its high-quality products and use of manual techniques for working leather goods. Louis Vuitton has now reached its fifth generation, building an international reputation as a high quality and creative producer. Its logo has spread worldwide via its ready-to-wear collection that was first introduced in 1997 by former creative director Marc Jacobs (Spindler, 1997).

Despite being created in a serial and industrialized manner, the production of Louis Vuitton continued to increase over the years, with its perception of prestige showing no signs of decline. It is because Louis Vuitton "enact virtual rarity tactics, constructing themselves as art" to avoid the commoditization effect (Kapferer, 2012, p. 453).

Louis Vuitton has long used a de-commoditization strategy through the use of arts (Gasparina, O'Brien, Igarashi, Luna, & Steele, 2009; Lee, Chen, & Wang, 2014; Riot, Chamaret, & Rigaud, 2013; Joy, Wang, Chan, Sherry, & Cui, 2014). Art collaborations such as the creation of the Louis Vuitton Contemporary Art Foundation, the increasing number of LV Cultural Spaces, and the recent establishment of a department dedicated to art and culture all collectively indicate that an art-based strategy has become prominent for the French luxury house.

After a historical overview illustrating the birth and evolution of Louis Vuitton, this case study will proceed with a description of its art-connected strategies and activities as well as those of its owner LVMH group (Louis Vuitton Moët Hennessy S.A.). Afterward, this chapter will focus on two peculiar art-based activities that the brand has realized in recent years: its collaboration with contemporary visual artists Takashi Murakami[2] and Yayoi Kusama[3] for the realization of the brand's limited edition collection for women in 2008 and 2012, respectively. "Successful artists can be thought of as brand managers, actively engaged in developing, nurturing, and promoting themselves as recognizable 'products' in the competitive cultural sphere" (Schroeder, 2005, p. 1292). In this sense, we will investigate how Murakami and Kusama each co-branded collections with Louis Vuitton involve different activities through an *artification* strategy that runs from the creation of a collection, the artist's sponsorship, and various patronage activities. Mainly, the analysis will describe communication activities managed by active participation from art institutions. These widespread collaborations effectively de-commoditized the Louis Vuitton brand by creating a virtual rarity through the limited collection. The communication activities related to these art-based collaborations were also able to bring Louis Vuitton products into established contemporary museums (Keller & Lehmann, 2003; Riot et al., 2013).

The collaboration with Murakami and Kusama were among the broadest artistic collaborations realized by Marc Jacobs, one of the main protagonists of the Louis Vuitton arts-based strategy. The chapter will end with recent art-based strategies implemented by Louis Vuitton's new creative director Nicolas Ghesquière and the intervention of new managerial and artistic directors.

The case was written using data from an interview with the Director of Louis Vuitton's Cultural Spaces in Paris, Marie-Ange Moulonguet (February, 2014), a site visit to the Louis Vuitton Foundation for Contemporary Art in Paris, several store visits in Italy and France in 2014 and 2016, articles published in trade and academic journals, books, the corporate website, and other mass media sources in English, French, and Italian.

OVERVIEW OF LVMH AND LOUIS VUITTON

Louis Vuitton is regarded as the first world luxury brand (Interbrand, 2016) and is the leading brand of the LVMH group. Later, we offer an overview of the LVMH group, followed by an overview specifically of the Louis Vuitton brand.

Overview of LVMH Group

LVMH group is one of the top three luxury conglomerates in the world, along with Kering (previously known as Pinault-Printemps-Redoute—PPR) and Richmond. The French multinational luxury goods company was founded in 1987, with a mission aimed at "representing the most refined qualities of the Western way of life around the world" (LVMH, 2016a). The group earned €35.7 billion in 2015 and reached an operated margin of 19%, thanks to its brand portfolio of seventy prestigious brands organized into five operating groups, including Fashion & Leather Goods, Selective Retailing Houses,[4] Wines & Spirits, Perfumes & Cosmetics, and Watches & Jewelry (Table 6.1) (Cavender & Kincade, 2014; LVMH, 2016b, 2016c). As Table 6.1 shows, the fashion & leather goods and selective retailing house categories account for approximately 35% and 31% of the revenue, respectively.

Since 1989, 46.6% of LVMH's shares belong to the Arnault family group, of which Bernard Arnault is the CEO. With more than 120,000 employees and an international retail network composed of 3,860 directly managed stores all over the world, the group has an established presence on every continent (Table 6.2).

The group operates a decentralized organization allowing brand autonomy and enhanced performance. Each brand maintains its unique identity, heritage, and expertise, all of which serve as cornerstones of long-term success. For group management, it is essential to preserve unique brand

Table 6.1 LVMH Revenues by Business Groups (€ millions)

Business Groups	2015	2014	2013
Fashion and Leather Goods	12,369	10,828	9,883
Selective Retailing	11,233	9,534	8,903
Wines and Spirits	4,603	3,973	4,173
Perfumes and Cosmetics	4,517	3,916	3,717
Watches and Jewelry	3,308	2,782	2,697
Other Activities and Eliminations	366	395	357
Total	35,664	30,638	29,016

Note: LV Fiscal year ended December 2015, LVMH (2015), p. 2

Table 6.2 LVMH Revenues and Stores by geographic region

Markets	Revenues (%)	Number of stores
Asia (excluding Japan)	27	951
United States	26	732
Europe (excluding France)	18	1,012
Other markets	12	276
France	10	482
Japan	7	407

Note: Developed by the authors based on LVMH (2015), p. 2

values while helping companies embrace new ideas and initiatives. At the group level, one of LVMH's strategic vectors is controlling the distribution of products, particularly for luxury Fashion and Leather Goods units. This allows the group to benefit from distribution margins, guarantee strict control of brand image, and create closer contact with its customers.

To meet these objectives, LVMH has created an international network of exclusive boutiques under the aegis of its Fashion and Leather Goods brands, which included 1,566 stores as of December 31, 2015. Fashion and leather goods constituted €12.3 billion in 2015, accounting for 34% of the group's turnover as reported by their official website. The primary markets for fashion and leather goods are France (9%), the rest of Europe (22%), the United States (22%), Japan (11%), the rest of Asia (28%), and other markets (8%). Bernard Arnault's formula for managing the LVMH group, specifically Louis Vuitton, consists of defining and shaping a brand image deeply rooted in high quality. The entire sales staff is sent to Paris to receive appropriate training, and employees are encouraged to understand the company's history and culture, along with the essence of the brand represented by the most refined art of travel[5] (Masè, 2016).

Louis Vuitton dominates the fashion and leather goods segment by reaching billions of customers as the flagship brand of the group. Its mission focuses on 'creative passion' and being a symbol of elegance and creativity by realizing dreams that cross tradition and modernity. It, therefore, frames its core values using concepts such as creativity and innovation, state-of-the-art product quality, and an invaluable brand trademark appeal. The next will give the primary information about the Louis Vuitton brand.

Overview of Louis Vuitton

The high dynamism of the global group is driven by the exceptional appeal of the Louis Vuitton brand, its efficiency in strategic development, and its long-standing presence worldwide. The prestigious French lifestyle, authentic know-how, and well-managed distribution network are all factors that have fueled Louis Vuitton's dynamism, a quality unscathed by the profound changes that occurred in company management in earlier years. After sixteen years, Marc Jacobs left his position as artistic director of the House in 2013 to focus on his namesake brand, in which LVMH has a majority stake (Menkes & Wilson, 2013). Furthermore, in 2014, former CEO Yves Carcelle passed away after more than twenty years of activity, dealing a severe blow to the strategy of the brand. The year 2015 became an important year for both the creative and managerial sides of the LVMH flagship-brand, bringing in a new creative designer in Nicolas Ghesquière and a new CEO in Michael Burke.

The brand's image is built on the idea of excellence based on traditional craftsmanship along with the "Made in France" production pattern. A strong focus is placed on sales: the products are sold without any promotional offers in 446 exclusive stores located in 52 countries. The overall strategy is based on sophistication and personalization because Louis Vuitton prioritizes the client above all. This attitude is reflected in their product offer, which has been diversified since 2011: special order or bespoke options are now available in the leather goods, footwear, and ready-to-wear categories. Fig. 6.1 shows a Louis Vuitton Flagship store in Paris that displays personalization tools used by sales associates for inscribing a customer's name.

Additionally, they have launched a new high-end leather goods line that can be fully personalized so that customers, under the guidance of a sales associate, can create a unique bag that reflects their personality. For men,

Fig. 6.1   Personalization space at the Louis Vuitton flagship store in Paris (*Note*: Photographed by Stefania Masè in June 2016. Personalization tools used by sales associates for inscribing a customer's name)

Louis Vuitton has created made-to-order footwear, a belt service, and a collection of evening ready-to-wear garments that can also be personalized (LVMH, 2011). Attention toward personalization has its precedents, as their famous trunks used to be sold as special orders for customers who wanted to differentiate themselves.

Regarding production, Louis Vuitton uses third parties only to supplement its manufacturing capacity and achieve production flexibility. There are seventeen leather goods manufacturing shops for Louis Vuitton trunk-maker: twelve in France,[6] three in Spain, and two in the United States (San Dimas, near Los Angeles), which provide most of the brand's production. All development and production processes for Louis Vuitton's footwear line are handled at its site in Fiesso d'Artico, Italy.

Louis Vuitton trunk-maker depends on outside suppliers for most of its leather and raw materials. Even though a significant proportion of the raw materials are purchased from a small number of suppliers, these materials could be obtained from other sources if necessary to limit dependence on specific suppliers.

Various surveys have shown that Louis Vuitton commands strong brand awareness all over the world (Cavender & Kincade, 2014; Interbrand, 2016). However, brand building in the luxury business remains a complex task. Store design and customer service reflect the company's traditions. Additionally, the company has consistently pursued a luxury pricing strategy of high markups, limited availability, and few if any markdowns, so as not to de-evaluate the brand in the eyes of customers. The next paragraph will describe some milestones in Louis Vuitton's history.

HISTORY OF LOUIS VUITTON

The company takes its name from its founder, a nineteenth-century Frenchman who had served as an apprentice trunk-maker to prominent households, including that of Napoleon III of France. Louis Vuitton was only 16-years-old when he arrived in Paris to work as an apprentice for Monsieur Maréchal. He learned the tradition of fabricating specialized products that require artisanal skills and customization based on clients' wishes. After seventeen years of experience, in 1854 Louis Vuitton opened his workshop at 4 Rue Neuve-des-Capucines in Paris (close to the Place Vendôme). One year afterward, he established a store in London and the first atelier in Asnières (northeast of Paris). This location today hosts the Vuitton family residence and the private family museum (Viguie-Desplaces, 2015). The Asnières workshop still makes exclusive products today, 170 craftsmen work there, creating special orders for clients all over the world.

In 1888, Vuitton produced his first classic damier signature pattern, a checkerboard print of contrasting light and dark brown squares. After he passed away in 1892, his son Georges Vuitton took over the company, taking it to new heights as the first "designer label" on a product. The company continued to grow and expand, and in 1914, the Louis Vuitton building opened on Champs-Elysées in Paris. The company has always pursued strategies of international expansion to satisfy the needs of a worldwide clientele and has often pioneered new foreign markets. In 1978, its first official stores were opened in Tokyo and Osaka, Japan, followed by the creation of Louis Vuitton Japan and the opening of a freestanding store in Ginza in 1981. Just after three years, it established a store in Seoul, South Korea. Most notably, in 1992, Louis Vuitton opened its first store in Beijing, China, being the first European luxury company to enter the market.

The 1980s were profitable years for Louis Vuitton. In 1983, the company sponsored the America's Cup preliminaries. Three years later, the company created the Louis Vuitton Foundation for opera and music. Also in 1986, the central Paris store moved from Avenue Marceau to the classier Avenue Montaigne. In 1984, at the urging of financial director Joseph Lafont, the company sold stock to the public on the Paris and New York exchanges. In June 1987, a USD $4 billion merger was effected between Louis Vuitton and Moët-Hennessy, which allowed the former to expand its investments in the luxury business while saving Moët-Hennessy from the threat of takeover.

The merger respected the autonomy of each company regarding management and subsidiaries. In 1997, the visionary designer Marc Jacobs began his role as Artistic Director of Louis Vuitton, and the company entered the world of ready-to-wear (Frankel, 2012). By commissioning artists, Louis Vuitton utilized their cutting-edge design ideas for signature products, creating must have status symbols. Always leading the avant-garde trends of fashion without compromising traditional craftsmanship, Louis Vuitton now participates in other creative spheres, its product portfolio covering articles for both men and women, as well as luggage and other leather goods, ready-to-wear clothing and accessories, shoes, watches, jewelry, sunglasses, travel books, and writing materials. Its range of handbags and briefcases is most popular. In addition to its products, Louis Vuitton offers a variety of services including special orders, customization, and product care repairs.

Louis Vuitton today enjoys an international reputation as a high quality and creative producer, preserving the past yet oriented toward the future. In addition to their historical heritage, another company value is its spirit of responsibility toward customers and communities as expressed through activities supporting corporate social responsibility and the sustainability of art and culture.

A Luxury Strategy Based on Arts and Artistic Collaborations

The LVMH group and the brand Louis Vuitton demonstrated their interest in the support of artistic and cultural activities and initiatives related to education, culture, and creativity in their traditional and contemporary expressions. As stated by Bernard Arnault, chairman and CEO of LVMH, "support for the arts and culture figures is at the very heart of our business model. Right from the creation of our Group, I made it clear that this is a strategic priority for our development. This commitment embodies the values our Houses all share – savoir-faire, excellence and creativity – and anchors them in their artistic, cultural and social environment." (LVMH, 2016d).

This attention to artistic heritage and culture has led to LVMH's global sponsorships and philanthropic activities, from the restoration of historical monuments to the support of collections at major museums, as well as contribution to an exhibition of young contemporary artists (LVMH, 2015). Art-connected activities are specifically implemented through time by the flagship brand, as shown in the following figure (Fig. 6.2).

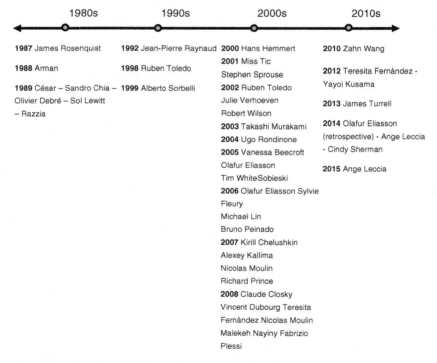

Fig. 6.2   Timeline of LV's collaboration with artists (*Note*: Elaborated by the authors. The timeline shows the main art-based collaboration between the artists listed and Louis Vuitton brand. The activities refer to sponsorship, retail exhibition, and product collaborations.)

As shown in Fig. 6.2, the relationship between Art & Business for Louis Vuitton strengthened during the 1990s, thanks especially to Marc Jacobs. A lover of contemporary and Pop art, Marc Jacobs invited artists to join forces with Louis Vuitton in various ways: designing showcases, art installations for retail, and exhibitions at the sales points. However, Marc Jacobs could not have implemented such a complex relationship with the arts were it not for the support of two other key players. The first was Bernard Arnault, a collector of contemporary art who initiated an operation for the rebirth of the flagship company to transform it into the ultimate expression of modern luxury. The other key player was Yves Carcelle, CEO of the French luxury brand until his death on August 31, 2014 (Crivelli, 2014). Yves Carcelle was the leading supporter of Louis Vuitton's collaborations with internationally renowned artists enlisted through Marc Jacobs. He also actively supported the opening of Louis Vuitton Cultural Spaces in the major capitals of the world and the LV Foundation for Contemporary Art, for which he was designated the first CEO (Crivelli, 2012a).

The company's collaborations with artists are evidence of a larger project of strategic brand identity building. Art can influence the customer's mindset of a brand (e.g., thoughts, feelings, experiences, images, perceptions, beliefs, and attitudes). The value of the brand ultimately depends on consumers, and communication activities influence the consumers' "mindset"—what they know and feel about it (Keller & Lehmann, 2003). Louis Vuitton's art-based activities comprise its *artification* strategy that aims to increase the perceived exclusiveness and prestige of luxury brands in the eyes of consumers via art-based activities. Bernard Arnault, Marc Jacobs, and Yves Carcelle incorporated artistic collaborations into the brand's DNA, increasing its prestige and exclusivity through arts by transforming it into one of the most famous luxury brands (Crivelli, 2014).

An analysis of Louis Vuitton's collaborations with artists is not always limited to spot collaborations, but can also include long-lasting relationships. Some artists are indicated as friends of the Maison through their connections with the history and evolution of the luxury brand (Louis Vuitton, 2016a). Such relationships have led LV to purchase or commission pieces of artwork by the Maison that are then exhibited in retail spaces or production plants or preserved in the main collection company (Louis Vuitton, 2016b). In other cases, artists are called to exhibit their work at Louis Vuitton's Cultural Spaces or to give live performances at commercial spaces. The following paragraphs will give pertinent examples about the activities managed by Louis Vuitton regarding the company's relationship with art.

Arts Exhibitions in Retail Spaces

LV displays art at its mono-brand retail spaces. In 2006, the brand exhibited a work by Danish contemporary artist Olafur Eliasson titled "Eye See You" (Bonacorsi, 2014; Eliasson, 2015). This initiative proved risky because the art was displayed in the brand's windows, limiting product visibility during the busy Christmas shopping period. Various works of other artists were displayed in the windows of the Louis Vuitton flagship worldwide. One provocative art exhibition was the live performance of Italian artist Vanessa Beecroft for the Louis Vuitton Parisian flagship store inauguration in 2005 (Lifestyle Navigator, 2005).

Another means by which art partners with mono-brand retail LV spaces is through the library sections. In these spaces, art books are exhibited and sold together with well-recognized LV city guides and enriched by photographs of famous international artists. Customers can also find books about ongoing exhibitions at the LV cultural spaces, located in areas adjacent to commercial showrooms in Paris, Tokyo, and Munich (Figs. 6.3 and 6.4).

Louis Vuitton Cultural Spaces

Louis Vuitton Cultural Spaces are sites dedicated to art exhibition, located at the top of LV flagship stores in Paris, Tokyo, and Monaco. Due to their connection to retail areas, consumers can visit the Cultural Space while shopping. These areas are similar to art galleries, functioning as a point of encounter between artists and potential buyers and communicating with the primary target audience of the brand: the international cultural élite. The brand presents itself as a cultural agent rather than as a producer of luxury goods, by strengthening its position in the international artistic scene/market through direct contact with artistic experts. By such means, Louis Vuitton presents itself as a cultural institution (Masè, 2016).

Louis Vuitton Foundation for Contemporary Art

The newest point of contact between Louis Vuitton and the world of art is the Louis Vuitton Foundation for Contemporary Art at the Bois

Fig. 6.3 Louis Vuitton store in Montenapoleone Street, Milan, the best-known fashion street in Italy (*Note*: Photographed by Elena Cedrola in March 2016)

de Boulogne in Paris, opened in 2014. The inauguration of a contemporary art museum directly managed by the brand further confirmed the brand's involvement as a patron of the arts (Fig. 6.5). The structure is an award-winning architecture project created by Frank

Fig. 6.4 A bookshop at Louis Vuitton flagship store at Champs Elysées, Paris (*Note*: Photographed by Stefania Masè in June 2016)

Ghery to preserve French and international contemporary artworks. The foundation holds a permanent collection and hosts cultural events to increase public awareness about Louis Vuitton's support for art and culture (Figs. 6.6a and b).

Arts Collaboration with Renowned Visual Artists for Limited Collections

Louis Vuitton is known for the variety and intensity of artistic collaborations used for its collections. In 1988, a series of silk scarves were commissioned to artists Sol LeWitt or Arman (Gasparina et al., 2009). The artists Stephen Sprouse in 2001 and Richard Prince in 2008 participated in Louis Vuitton collections, working alongside Marc Jacobs and enriching products with their creations inhering in the Visual Arts. The

Fig. 6.5 Foundation Louis Vuitton pour l'Art Contemporain (*Note*: Photographed by Stefania Masè in September 2015)

most important collaborations for the design of LV collections may be those with Japanese artists Takashi Murakami in 2003 and 2008, and Yayoi Kusama in 2012. These two collaborations are examples of co-branding, given the vastness of the partnerships leading to the realization of the entire product line (Schroeder, 2005). Extensive communication has always linked the LV logo with the distinguishing marks of the two Japanese artists. The next paragraphs will describe the two co-branding collaborations in more detail.

LV and Takashi Murakami

Undoubtedly, Louis Vuitton's artistic collaboration with Takashi Murakami was one of the most decisive collaborations that the brand established (Lee et al., 2014). The artist has collaborated several times with the luxury brand since 2003. Marc Jacobs first saw Murakami's work during a performance at the Foundation Cartier in Paris in 2002, where the Japanese artist was presenting a personal retrospective.

The following year, LV presented its first collection resulting from the collaboration between Marc Jacobs and Takashi Murakami. This collection involved a reworking of the traditional Louis Vuitton logo in several variations based on Murakami's creations. It included the creation of an entire collection, from scarves and shoes to accessories and bags. Understandably, Murakami's intervention modified various visual elements of the brand that could have potentially detrimental consequences to the recognition of a brand that has built its reputation on elegance and

Fig. 6.6 (a)   Foundation Louis Vuitton pour l'Art Contemporain, artist Daniel Buren installation (*Note*: Photographed by Stefania Masè in June 2016)

Fig. 6.6 (b) Foundation Louis Vuitton pour l'Art Contemporain, artist Daniel Buren installation (*Note*: Photographed by Stefania Masè in June 2016)

classical taste. However, these possible adverse reactions arising from collaborations with visual artists have not been verified (Luke, 2015).

In 2008, the relationship between Takashi Murakami and Louis Vuitton reached an even higher level. During a retrospective dedicated to the artist at the Museum of Contemporary Art (MOCA) in Los Angeles, the artist took the opportunity to install Louis Vuitton's pop-up store at the heart of the exhibition, as if it were a work of art itself rather than a commercial section of the museum. The temporary store exhibited the collection created in collaboration with the artist, and visitors could buy the products displayed. This provocation caused a scandal in the American art community, despite it being supposedly more open to the relationship between Art and Business than were most European art communities (Martorella, 1996; Wu, 2003). Such symbiosis between Art and Business within a museum was thought to be a major transgression of artistic values.

The experimental collaboration between Marc Jacobs and Takashi Murakami rejuvenated the brand and its target audience, such that the products combining Vuitton & Murakami became best sellers (Riot et al., 2013).

LV and Yayoi Kusama

Due to the success of the Murakami collections in 2012, Louis Vuitton repeated the co-branding strategy with another internationally renowned Japanese artist named Yayoi Kusama. Marc Jacobs met Yayoi Kusama during his trip to Japan in 2006. The now 89-year-old visionary artist has built her philosophy on the idea that "The earth is only a small polka dot in the universe" (Crivelli, 2012b). From this statement, one may understand why almost all of her work is characterized by the distinctive use of dot patterns. These dot patterns repeated endlessly represent the first point of convergence between the artist and Louis Vuitton, a brand known for its repeated monogram.

The project with Yayoi Kusama was circumscribed at the start before expanding over time to encompass sponsorship activities, window designs for flagship stores, and the creation of new products for an entire collection, ranging from clothes and shoes to bags and accessories. Yayoi Kusama and her works had long been the subject of major retrospectives organized in leading museums around the world (Crivelli, 2012b; Degli Innocenti, 2012; Kusama, 2016). After she and Marc Jacobs first met in 2006, she requested a sponsorship in 2011 to Hervé Mikaeloff, the art expert and curator of LVMH and the Louis Vuitton Foundation (Menkes & Wilson, 2013). They conceived of the idea of a capsule collection[7] signed by LV and Kusama that can exploit the beneficial synergy of sponsorship activities. The collaboration materialized in 2011 when the capsule 2012 collection was being planned. Simultaneous sponsorships from Louis Vuitton were established for Yayoi Kusama's retrospective at the Tate Gallery in London and the Whitney Museum in New York City. They were variations on two retrospectives previously hosted at the Centre Pompidou in Paris and the Museo Reina Sofia in Madrid (Crivelli, 2012b). For the exhibition at the Tate Gallery in London, visited by 186,551 people, Vuitton offered support for associated events and parallel programs (Menkes & Wilson, 2013).

As confirmed by Hervé Mikaeloff, a collaboration between Yayoi Kusama and Louis Vuitton was launched in the summer of 2012 and was probably the largest artistic collaboration held by a luxury or fashion company. Two contracts were composed—one for the design of nearly 1500 showcase windows by Yayoi Kusama (Figs. 6.7a and b) and another contract for the collections she realized with Marc Jacobs scheduled for July and October 2012 (Judah, 2013). Table 6.3 summarizes Louis Vuitton's collaborations with Takashi Murakami and Yayoi Kusama.

These artistic collaborations comprise a mix of patronage, cooperation, and sponsorship activities. They reached higher levels of involvement than did previous collaborations. The support of the brand's entire strategic direction led to cooperation with the two Japanese artists for the purpose of appealing to younger consumers (Riot et al., 2013). Through these artistic collaborations, Louis Vuitton wanted to reach new consumers through communication dedicated to the colorful and fresh design of its collection.

After recent changes that affected the managerial and artistic direction of the French Maison, the LV *artification* strategy has evolved as well toward a focus on international recognition, as described in the next paragraph.

Fig. 6.7 (a)   Yayoi Kusama statue with bag on Louis Vuitton window at Louis Vuitton Flagship store, Champs Elysées, Paris (*Note*: Photographed by Stefania Masè in September 2012)

Fig. 6.7 (b)   Yayoi Kusama artwork on Louis Vuitton window at Louis Vuitton Flagship store, Champs Elysées, Paris (*Note*: Photographed by Stefania Masè in September 2012)

LV's Recent *Artification* Activities

In 2014, the artistic direction of the Maison was assigned to Nicolas Ghesquière when Marc Jacobs took over the reins of his eponymous brand. Ghesquière's new role will be to relaunch the ready-to-wear lines that were introduced in 1997 by Marc Jacobs that currently represent only 5% of the brand's total sales (Matzeu, 2015). An increase in the percentage of prêt-à-porter sales is linked to a criticism of commoditization toward Louis Vuitton; co-branding may allow it to increase sales and raise brand awareness without undermining perceived luxury for consumers. For example, in 2014, six world-renowned artists, architects, and designers presented a tribute to Louis Vuitton's monogram. These figures were Cindy Sherman, Rei Kawakubo, Frank Ghery, Karl Lagerfeld, Cristian Laboutin, and Marc Newson. The collection was linked to some interesting external activity. During the days

Table 6.3 A summary of *artification* strategy with Takashi Murakami and Yahoi Kusama

	Art-based activities
Product design	Through the art-based collections, LV offers highly recognizable products that are profoundly different from the classical Louis Vuitton collection, such as the colorful and witty design by Takashi Murakami, or the bright polka dots by Yayoi Kusama. All those collections are targeted to appeal young consumers; this is why prices were "on target" with a €225 for a slip-swimsuit and €215 for an infinity dots scarf, very low-level price for LV (Verde, 2012).
Advertising	The art-based collections are communicated via unconventional advertising, as the "Superflat first love" video Takashi Murakami realized to advertise its collection. The video was a communication tool based on a cartoon-animated style, which totally differentiated itself from the familiar luxury brand's sophisticated communication (Murakami, 2016).
Sponsorship	Takashi Murakami retrospective at Museum of Contemporary Art in Los Angeles; LV and Murakami limited editions bags were exhibited and sold inside of a major artistic institution, while outside of the museum the same bags were marketed as counterfeited products (Riot et al., 2013). The discussed pop-up store opened inside of the Museum and the sale on the street of the same as counterfeiting pieces was an unusual form of anti-luxury communication.
	Yayoi Kusama retrospective at Whitney Museum for contemporary art in New York in July 2012; the Museum was decorated with big balls and red balloons with white polka dots, recalling the pattern of LV & Kusama collection.
Pop Up Stores and Window Displays	Special design for store windows, worldwide;
	Pop up stores dedicated to the Yayoi Kusama collection;
	Pop up stores dedicated to the Takashi Murakami collection at MOMA;
	Windows-exhibition at LV retail spaces

Note: Developed by the authors

of the Foundation's opening at the Jardins d'Acclimatation in Paris, Frank Gehry (also the author of a bag belonging to 2014 collection) created the windows of the Louis Vuitton shops while the Centre Pompidou museum featured a retrospective of his works (Luxury Daily, 2014).

Nicolas Ghesquière is not as known in the art sphere as Marc Jacobs, who is a collector before being a designer. The LV art-based strategy aims to converge the image of the new artistic director to the arts via *artifica-tion* (Dion & Arnould, 2011). An example of this strategy is the London series 3, fashion shows in London that merge the fashion runway with an exhibition devoted to describing the talent and inspiration of the Maison's new creative director (Louis Vuitton, 2016c).

The 2016 collection, realized by the creative director of LV, exhibits a fresh and colored design aimed at appealing to a higher and younger cross-section of the population, as the Kusama and Murakami collections had intended. As shown in the pictures in Fig. 6.8, the new collection spring summer 2016 cover and re-elaborates the classic LV logo as it was done initially with artists as previously described. This time, the logo and pattern were not modified by an external artist but by the designer of the French Luxury house (Figs. 6.8a and b).

Fig. 6.8 (a)   Nicolas Ghesquière SS 2016 collection at Louis Vuitton Flagship store, Champs Elysées, Paris (*Note*: Photographed by Stefania Masè in June 2016)

Fig. 6.8 (b)   Nicolas Ghesquière SS 2016 collection at Louis Vuitton Flagship store, Champs Elysées, Paris (*Note*: Picture taken by Stefania Masè in June 2016)

DISCUSSION AND IMPLICATION

Management seems to have now recognized and accepted the fact that art constitutes a positive value for entrepreneurial activity (Alexander, 1996; Martorella, 1996). For this reason, investing in art has proven to be a viable strategy in building cultural infrastructure favorable to a brand that strengthens its image (Hetsroni & Tukachinsky, 2005). Luxury branding is increasingly utilizing art-based strategies known as *artification*. This approach corresponds to convergent activities that partner the brand with the art world in a coherent and synergistic manner. Connection with the art world through *artification* helps luxury brands maintain their prestige and exclusivity, despite mass production and widespread availability at retail stores throughout the world. Basically, an art-based strategy preserves "rarity" for luxury items by connecting/lifting their image to the status of an art piece.

The main luxury brands, such as Chanel, Hermès, and Prada, adhere to a strategy focusing on arts (Weidemann & Hennings, 2013). All of these luxury brands manage different points of contact with the arts, such as sponsorships, philanthropic activities, collaborations with artists for collections and advertising, and corporate collections. However, they have not yet reached the level of Louis Vuitton's strategy, especially regarding the creation of artist capsule-collections (Masè, 2016). In fact, the luxury conglomerate LVMH pursues an exemplary art-based strategy. It manages connections with the art world through various activities such as the "Monumenta," an exhibition in the Grand Palais that has shown artwork each year since 2007 of the most recognized contemporary international artists (Grand Palais, 2016). At the same time, patronage activities stimulate curiosity and passion for art and culture among young students by promoting activities at school. Other initiatives to support young talent include the LVMH Prize for Young Fashion Designers, the Institut des Métiers d'Excellence for developing careers in traditional craftsmanship, and the Hyeres International Festival of Fashion and Photography, which is "designed to promote young creative talent in the fields of fashion and photography" (LVMH, 2016b).

LVMH infuses an "artistic" aura into all of its 70 luxury brands, but this art-based strategy reaches its maximum expression in the flagship brand LV. Over the past twenty years, LV has expanded its support activities to the arts through philanthropy, sponsorship, and artistic collaborations that take the form of co-branding for the realization of limited collections (Schroeder, 2005). The realization of ready-to-wear capsules collections with artists would allow luxury brands to increase sales while also avoiding the trap of commoditization (Riot et al., 2013). For the collaborations with Takashi Murakami and Yayoi Kusama, this anti-commoditization effect seems to have been successful, as limited collection products have become cult products, also sold via art auction houses as limited pieces (Sotheby's, 2016).

The presence of art experts inside the company has enabled a smoother collaboration with museums and a synergy of communication with the art world. Some examples of art-lovers within Louis Vuitton are Hervé Mikaeloff (the internal curator), Marc Jacobs, Yves Carcelle, Bernard

Arnault, and our interviewee Marie-Ange Moulonguet. These experts fully sustain the activities of artists and organize exhibition activities that run, for example, in the Louis Vuitton Foundation for Contemporary Art.

The art-based strategies of Louis Vuitton will continuously evolve to increase ready-to-wear sales to a more profitable percentage, particularly by realizing capsule collections with artists to avoid commoditization. Due to recent structural changes in Louis Vuitton's management and artistic direction, corporate strategies concerning art-related strategies will soon change as well, orienting even more toward culture and the arts (Masè, 2016). As indicated by the Director of LV Cultural Space in Paris, there will soon be more Cultural Spaces in the world. The individual activities of the new spaces will fall under the leadership of the new Department of Art & Culture and the director of Cultural Spaces in Tokyo, Christine Vendredi-Auzanneau (Rodriguez-Ely, 2014). Still, art and culture will continue to serve as integral parts to a strategic activity at the center of the brand, as stated in the company mission.

Giving consumers the possibility of buying a luxury product and enjoying an art exhibition in retail spaces, as well as appreciating renowned artists at the LV Foundation, puts the French Luxury house on track to becoming the most prominent luxury brand in the contemporary art and luxury meta market.

NOTES

1. Commoditization is a threat throughout a company: "its competitive position being eroded so that it can no longer command a premium price in its market. Whether caused by a new low-cost competitor (such as fashion's Zara), new product innovation [...] or the introduction of multiple substitutes and imitators" (D'Aveni, 2010, p. 2).
2. One of the most acclaimed artists to emerge from post-war Asia, Takashi Murakami—the Warhol of Japan—is known for his contemporary Pop synthesis of fine art and popular culture. Born in Tokyo in 1962, the artist still operates in the Japanese capital (Artsy, 2016a).
3. Avant-garde Japanese artist Yayoi Kusama was an influential figure in the post-war New York art scene, staging provocative happenings and exhibiting works such as her "Infinity Nets." Born in 1929 in Matsumoto City, the Japanese artist is still active in Tokyo (Artsy, 2016b).
4. Operating in Europe, the Americas, Asia, and the Middle East, the selective retailing houses are active in two spheres: retail designed for international traveler customers (DFS and Miami Cruiseline), and selective retailing

concepts represented by Sephora, the most innovative name in the world of beauty, and Le Bon Marché Rive Gauche, the department store with a unique atmosphere located in Paris.

5. Journeys are one of the core essences of LV brands. As travelling is a style of life, LV presents itself as a brand that transforms the act of travelling into an art.

6. A vast majority of the workforce is composed of skilled operators called maroquiniers, representing the direct workforce.

7. A capsule collection is essentially a condensed version of a designer's version, often limited edition, which transcends seasons and trends (Morton, 2016).

REFERENCES

Alexander, V. D. (1996). From philanthropy to funding: The effects of corporate and public support on American art museums. *Poetics, 24*(2–4), 87–129. doi:10.1016/0304-422X(95)00003-3

Artsy. (2016a). Takashi Murakami. Retrieved from https://www.artsy.net/artist/takashi-murakami

Artsy. (2016b). Yayoi Kusama. Retrieved from https://www.artsy.net/artist/yayoi-kusama

Bonacorsi, I. (2014). Olafur Eliasson: Contact. *Domus web*. Retrieved from http://www.domusweb.it/it/arte/2014/12/18/olafur_eliasson_contact.html

Cavender, R. C., & Kincade, D. H. (2014). Management of a luxury brand: Dimensions and sub-variables from a case study of LVMH. *Journal of Fashion Marketing and Management, 18*(2), 231–248. doi: 10.1108/JFMM-03-2013-0041

Crivelli, G. (2012a). Louis Vuitton apre la prima maison a Shangai. Il ceo Carcelle: Le prossime tappe sono Pechino e Hangzhou. Retrieved from http://www.moda24.ilsole24ore.com/art/retail-web/2012-07-18/louis-vuitton-apre-prima-110957.php?uuid=AbB61h9F

Crivelli, G. (2012b). A New York Louis Vuitton cresce con l'arte di Yayoi Kusama. Retrieved from http://www.moda24.ilsole24ore.com/art/stili-tendenze/2012-07-11/york-louis-vuitton-cresce-164931.php?uuid=AbB7pD6F

Crivelli, G. (2014). Addio a Carcelle, pioniere e mecenate che ha creato la 'nuova' Louis Vuitton. Retrieved from http://www.moda24.ilsole24ore.com/art/industria-finanza/2014-09-02/-carcelle-pioniere-e-mecenate-che-ha-creato-nuova-louis-vuitton-114223.php?uuid=ABRXdcpB

D'Aveni, R. (2010). *Beating the commodity trap: How to maximize your competitive position and increase your pricing power*. Boston, MA: Harvard Business Publishing.

Daily, L. (2014). Louis Vuitton teases art center opening with multimedia runway show. Retrieved from http://www.luxurydaily.com/louis-vuitton-teases-art-center-opening-with-multimedia-runway-show/

Degli Innocenti, N. (2012). Yayoi Kusama invade Selfridges. Retrieved from http://www.moda24.ilsole24ore.com/art/retail-web/2012-08-22/yayoi-kusama-invade-selfridges-160046.php?uuid=AbAPD9RG&fromSearch

Dion, D., & Arnould, E. (2011). Retail luxury strategy: Assembling charisma through art and magic. *Journal of Retailing, 87*(4), 502–520. doi:10.1016/j.jretai.2011.09.001

Dubois, B., Laurent, G., & Czellar, S. (2001). Consumer rapport to luxury: Analyzing complex and ambivalent attitudes. *Les Cahiers de Recherche, 33*(1), 1–56. Retrieved from http://www.hec.fr/var/fre/storage/original/application/5ecca063454eb4ef8227d08506a8673b.pdf

Eliasson, O. (2015). Eye see you. Retrieved from http://olafureliasson.net/archive/artwork/WEK100607/eye-see-you

Frankel, S. (2012, February 11). An American in Paris: Marc Jacobs' 15 years at Louis Vuitton. *Independent*. Retrieved from http://www.independent.co.uk/life-style/fashion/features/an-american-in-paris-marc-jacobs-15-years-at-louis-vuitton-6668107.html

Gasparina, J., O'Brien, G., Igarashi, T., Luna, I., & Steele, V. (2009). *Louis Vuitton: Art, fashion and architecture*. New York: Rizzoli.

Heinich, N., & Shapiro, R. (2012). *De l'artification—Enquêtes sur le passage à l'art. Cas de figure*. Paris: EHESS.

Hetsroni, A., & Tukachinsky, R. H. (2005). The use of fine art in advertising: A survey of creatives and content analysis of advertisements. *Journal of Current Issues & Research in Advertising (CTC Press), 27*(1), 93–107. doi:10.1080/10641734.2005.10505176

Interbrand. (2016). Best global brands 2015. Retrieved from http://interbrand.com/best-brands/best-global-brands/2015/ranking/

Joy, A., Wang, J. J., Chan, T.-S., Sherry Jr., J. F., & Cui, G. (2014). M(art)worlds: Consumer perceptions of how luxury brand stores become art institutions. *Journal of Retailing, 90*(3), 347–364. doi:10.1016/j.jretai.2014.01.002

Judah, H. (2013). Inside an artist collaboration. Retrieved from www.businessoffashion.com/articles/intelligence/inside-an-artist-collaboration

Kapferer, J. N. (2012). Abundant rarity: the key to luxury growth. *Business Horizons, 55*(5), 453–462. doi:10.1016/j.bushor.2012.04.002

Kapferer, J. N. (2014). The artification of luxury: from artisans to artists. *Business Horizons, 57*(3), 371–380. doi:10.1016/j.bushor.2013.12.007

Keller, K. L., & Lehmann, D. (2003). How do brands create value?. *Marketing Management, 12*(3), 26–31.

Kusama, Y. (2016). Information. Retrieved from http://www.yayoi-kusama.jp/e/information/

Lee, H. C., Chen, W. W., & Wang, C. W. (2014). The role of visual art in enhancing perceived prestige of luxury brands. *Marketing Letters, 26*(4), 593–606. doi:10.1007/s11002-014-9292-3

Luke, B. (2015, February 20). The many moods of Takashi Murakami. *Sotheby's*. Retrieved from http://www.sothebys.com/en/news-video/blogs/all-blogs/sotheby-s-magazine–march-2015/2015/02/takashi-murakami-louis-vuitton.html

LVMH. (2011). Investors publications. Retrieved from https://www.lvmh.com/investors/publications/

LVMH. (2015). Investors publications. Retrieved from https://www.lvmh.com/investors/publications/

LVMH. (2016a). Group about. Retrieved from https://www.lvmh.com/group/about-lvmh/the-lvmh-spirit/

LVMH. (2016b). Group about. Retrieved from https://www.lvmh.com/houses/#wines-spirits

LVMH. (2016c). Houses. Retrieved from https://www.lvmh.com/houses/

LVMH. (2016d). LVMH commitments art-culture. Retrieved from https://www.lvmh.com/group/lvmh-commitments/art-culture/

Martorella, R. (1996). *Arts and business: an international perspective on sponsorship*. Westport, CT: Greenwood Publishing Group.

Masè, S. (2016). *Art & business: From sponsorship and philanthropy to the contemporary process of artification*. Unpublished doctoral dissertation. Sorbonne & Macerata Universities, Paris.

Matzeu, E. (2015). Come va Nicolas Ghesquière da Louis Vuitton. Retrieved from http://www.ilpost.it/2015/10/09/nicolas-ghesquiere-louis-vuitton/

Menkes, S., & Wilson, E. (2013). Marc Jacobs to leave Louis Vuitton. *The New York Times*. Retrieved from http://www.nytimes.com/2013/10/02/fashion/marc-jacobs-to-leave-louis-vuitton.html?_r=0

Morton, C. (2016). Fashion A-Z. *Business of fashion*. Retrieved from https://www.businessoffashion.com/education/fashion-az/capsule-collections

Murakami, T. (2016). *Louis Vuitton x Takashi Murakami Superflat First Love* [Video file]. Retrieved from https://vimeo.com/5198631

Naukkarinen, O. (2012). Variations in artification. Retrieved from http://www.contempaesthetics.org/newvolume/pages/journal.php?volume=49

Navigator, L.. (2005). High heels—chez Louis Vuitton Paris. Retrieved from http://www.lifestylenavigator.de/?p=165

Palais, G. (2016). Monumenta 2016 Huang Yong Ping. Retrieved from http://www.grandpalais.fr/en/event/monumenta-2016-huang-yong-ping

Riot, E., Chamaret, C., & Rigaud, E. (2013). Murakami on the bag: Louis Vuitton's decommoditization strategy. *International Journal of Retail & Distribution Management, 41*(11/12), 919–939. doi:10.1108/IJRDM-01-2013-0010

Rodriguez-Ely, N. (2014). Culture is the word at Louis Vuitton. Retrieved from http://observatoire-art-contemporain.com/revue_decryptage/analyse_a_ decoder.php?langue=en&id=20120589

Schroeder, J. E. (2005). The artist and the brand. *European Journal of Marketing*, *39*(11/12), 1291–1305. doi:10.1108/03090560510623262

Sotheby's. (2016). The best of Louis Vuitton's artist collaborations.Retrieved from http://www.sothebys.com/en/news-video/slideshows/2015/louis-vuitton-birthday-best-artist-designer-collaborations.html#slideshow/2015. louis-vuitton-birthday-best-artist-designer-collaborations/7

Spindler, A. M. (1997, January 7). Vuitton and Jacobs seen in ready-to-wear deal. *The New York Times*. Retrieved from http://www.nytimes.com/1997/01/07/style/vuitton-and-jacobs-seen-in-ready-to-wear-deal.html

Verde, S. (2012). Cercate Yayoi Kusama? È da Vuitton. Retrieved from http://www.huffingtonpost.it/simone-verde/cercate-yayoi-kusama-e-da_b_1961100.html

Vigneron, F., & Johnson, L. W. (1999). A Review and a conceptual framework of prestige-seeking consumer behavior. *Academy of Marketing Science Review*, *1999*(1), 1–15.

Vigneron, F., & Johnson, L. W. (2004). Measuring perceptions of brand luxury. *Brand Management*, *11*(6), 484–506. doi:10.2466/pms.1991.72.1.329

Viguie-Desplaces, P. (2015). Louis Vuitton pose ses malles à Asnières-sur-Seine. Retrieved from www.lefigaro.fr/lifestyle/2015/06/29/30001-20150629ARTIFIG00268-louis-vuitton-poses-ses-mailles.php

Vuitton, Louis. (2016a). Gli Amici della Maison. Retrieved from http://it.louis vuitton.com/ita-it/arte/gli-amici-della-maison

Vuitton, Louis. (2016b). Art wall. Retrieved from http://eu.louisvuitton.com/eng-el/art/art-wall

Vuitton, Louis. (2016c). Series 3 exhibition London. Retrieved from http://fr. louisvuitton.com/fra-fr/mode/series-3-exhibition-london#/exhibition

Weidemann, K. P., & Henningss, N. (2013). *Luxury marketing a challenge for theory and practice*. Wiesbaden: Springer Gabler. doi:10.1007/978-3-8349-4399-6

Wu, C. T. (2003). *Privatizing culture: Corporate art intervention since the 1980s* (2nd ed.). London: Verso.

Stefania Masè is an adjunct professor (ATER - Attaché Temporaire d'Enseignement et de Recherche) at the University of Pau and the Adour Region, France, where she teaches marketing and international marketing. She is also a professor of Marketing Metrics at the University of Macerata, Italy. Her current research interests include luxury goods, consumer behavior, and marketing of culture and the arts.

Elena Cedrola is associate professor at the University of Macerata, Italy, where she teaches management and international marketing. She is also professor of International Marketing at the Catholic University of Milan, Italy. She was a visiting scholar at the Beijing Normal University (China) in 2014–2017, and at the Paris IV Sorbonne University (France) in 2014–2015. Dr. Cedrola's research areas are international management and marketing for small- and medium-sized enterprises. She has an extensive portfolio of intellectual contributions comprising of refereed journal publications, presentations, invited keynote speeches, lectures, and workshops. Her latest research focuses on country of origin in the industrial sectors.

INDEX

© The Author(s) 2017
B. Jin, E. Cedrola (eds.), *Fashion Branding and Communication*,
Palgrave Studies in Practice: Global Fashion Brand Management,
DOI 10.1057/978-1-137-52343-3